Best Easy Day Hikes
Oklahoma City

Help Us Keep This Guide Up to Date

Every effort has been made by the author and editors to make this guide as accurate and useful as possible. However, many things can change after a guide is published—trails are rerouted, regulations change, facilities come under new management, etc.

We would appreciate hearing from you concerning your experiences with this guide and how you feel it could be improved and kept up to date. While we may not be able to respond to all comments and suggestions, we'll take them to heart and we'll also make certain to share them with the author. Please send your comments and suggestions to the following address:

GPP
Reader Response/Editorial Department
PO Box 480
Guilford, CT 06437

Or you may e-mail us at:

editorial@GlobePequot.com

Thanks for your input, and happy trails!

Best Easy Day Hikes Series

Best Easy Day Hikes Oklahoma City

Gigi Ragland

FALCONGUIDES

GUILFORD, CONNECTICUT
HELENA, MONTANA

AN IMPRINT OF GLOBE PEQUOT PRESS

FALCONGUIDES®

FalconGuides is an imprint of Globe Pequot Press.
Falcon, FalconGuides, and Outfit Your Mind are registered trademarks of Morris Book Publishing, LLC.

Text design: Sheryl P. Kober
Project editor: Heather Santiago
Layout: Joanna Beyer
Maps: Daniel Lloyd © Morris Book Publishing, LLC

Library of Congress Cataloging-in-Publication Data is available on file.

ISBN 978-0-7627-6377-1

Printed in the United States of America

10 9 8 7 6 5 4 3 2 1

Contents

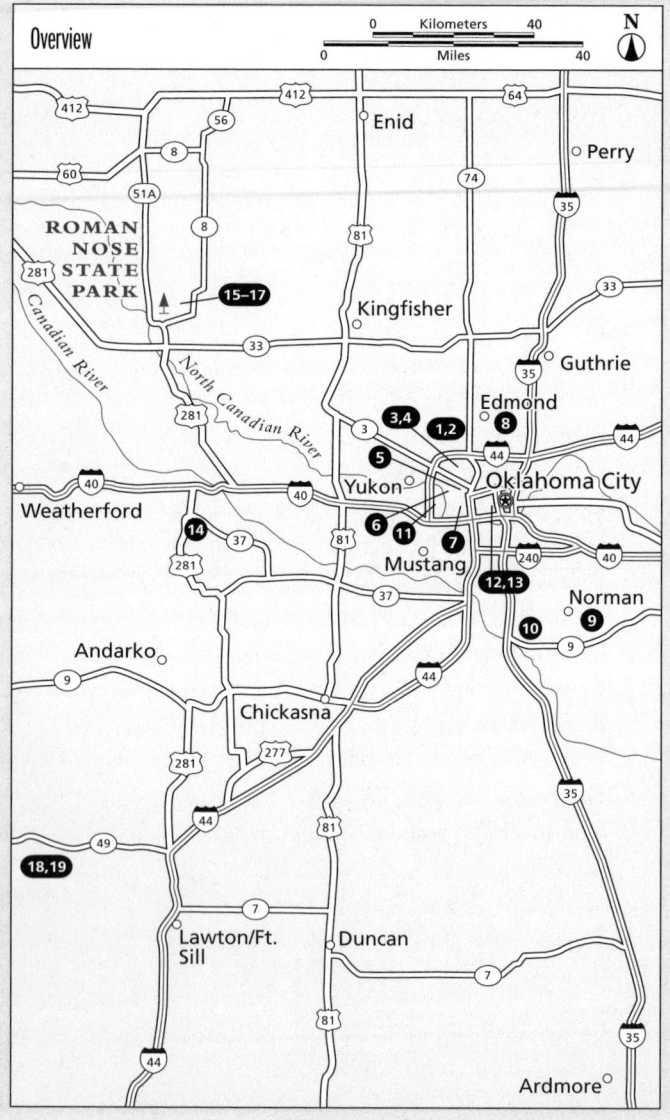

Overview

Acknowledgments

First, I would like to thank my editor, Jessica Haberman, for her patience and encouragement. And thanks to the Oklahoma Tourism and Recreation Department folks who offered their suggestions and support during the research of this book.

To my lifelong Oklahoma City friends, I greatly appreciate your hospitality and sharing your homes and hiking time with me. Thank you Beth and James Hooper, Danny Theisen, Kevin Mahoney, and Shannon Masterson.

Lastly, thank you to my husband, Mark Cerney, for his loving encouragement and for informing me of the University of Oklahoma Sooners football game scores during hikes.

Introduction

"You can take the girl out of the country, but you can't take the country out of the girl." I was born and raised in Oklahoma City and headed westward to California after college, like so many other pioneers of yesteryear in pursuit of their dreams. But the pride and pioneering spirit of being an Oklahoman has never left me.

The forty-sixth state offers a strong Indian and pioneer history; its heritage is evident in some of the stunning areas of the plains. The hikes in this book uncover my favorites within the Oklahoma City metro area and those parks within an hour's drive "as the crow flies" of the downtown area.

Much of the natural beauty of yesteryear's landscape can still be enjoyed today. The hikes in this book offer perspectives of natural history from the nineteenth century on into the present day with a variety of options for outdoor activities. There's more than meets the eye when deciding where to hike in Oklahoma City.

If you could go back in time to the nineteenth century, before Oklahoma was declared a state, the scene before you might look like this: vast tallgrass prairies that spread out into a sea of grassy waves, and herds of bison thundering across wide stretches of landscape along with herds of elk, deer, and wild cattle sniffing out grazing grounds along the never-ending dinner plate of the plains before them.

You might discover, as Native Americans did, pockets of rocky escarpments jutting upward amid the flat plains. Giant red rock canyon walls, sandstone, and sheer cliffs of shale, dolomite, and gypsum seemed to heave randomly out of the earth in the middle of no-man's-land. These canyon walls and barriers provided protection from the elements for tribes of Indians who made winter camps in places like Roman Nose State Park, named after the Comanche chief who settled there. Pioneers making their way toward California discovered the recuperating oasis the red rock canyons provided as well, often using the canyon valleys for a rest stop. At Red Rock State Park, you can still see the worn path of wagon-wheel ruts carved into the rock by the many brave men, women, and children making their way west.

And if you think Oklahoma City is just a big cow town, you'll find that it's much more. A visit to Stockyards City is worth the effort, but the city has plenty more to offer. Since 2000 Oklahoma City has undergone a renaissance of urban renewal, restoration, and renovation. The downtown area is thriving, providing a dynamic environment for its citizens and visitors. The Oklahoma River Trail featured in this guide was one of the projects of the expansive renewal programs invested in by the city. In the 1990s downtown Oklahoma City was not the urban playground it is today, with the addition of Bricktown, the Myriad Gardens renovation, and the city regentrification projects. There are plenty of walks to explore in the downtown area, including Hike 12, the Downtown Urban Museum Trail. Venture out with a map in your hand and see where the afternoon takes you.

Weather

Visitors can expect four seasons in the Plains state, with an average of 300 days of sunshine per year. So the odds are good that your outing will be sunny at some point. "If you don't like the weather in Oklahoma, wait a minute and it'll change," claimed the famous twentieth-century Oklahoma humorist Will Rogers. It says a lot about the state's change-able weather conditions, especially in the spring. Slashing rainstorms accompanied by tornado alerts occur suddenly and can be over in 5 minutes, giving way to a perfectly sunny spring day. So be prepared with rain gear and check for weather updates before heading out. Volatile weather can occur from mid-March through June, when tornadoes are most likely to make an appearance within "Tornado Alley." Even so, spring provides some of the best days to hike, adorning the metro area in colorful displays of wildflowers, green grassy meadows, leafy green trees, and a powder-blue sky, with average temperatures in the high sixties to low seventies Fahrenheit.

Summer temperatures range from the low nineties to one hundred degrees plus. August is typically the hottest month, with temperatures that can reach over one hundred degrees. The past few years have seen record heat in Oklahoma during summer. It's best to start out very early in the morning before the scorching temperatures hit their highs or plan hikes after sunset. Wear a hat, sunscreen, and sunglasses. Be sure to bring water along on your hike as dehydration is possible when hiking in very hot conditions.

Fall is an exceptionally long season, lasting from mid-September through November, and offers some of the best hiking conditions. High temperatures range in the seventies with comfortable low averages in the fifties. Be prepared for sudden weather changes like rain, sleet, or windy conditions. The profusion of autumnal colors during fall foliage high-lights any nature walk or hike with extraordinary beauty at this time of year. Winter is not the best time to hike, but there are a few days with great sunshine for getting outdoors. However, winter winds can make hiking chilly. Average temperatures can range from the forties to the fifties, but the windchill factor makes it seem much colder.

For updates on weather conditions, check local television and radio stations, or refer to these websites:

- National Weather Service Forecast Office, State of Oklahoma: www.ok.gov/redirect.php?link_id=90
- TravelOK.com: www.travelok.com/weather/

More information about Oklahoma's climate can be found at the Oklahoma Climatological Survey's website at http://climate.ok.gov. Monitor Oklahoma's weather at www.mesonet.org.

Wilderness Restrictions/Regulations

Trails managed by Oklahoma City Parks and Recreation Department include Lake Hefner Trails, Oklahoma River Trails, Bluff Creek Trail, Route 66 Park, Dolese Youth Park, and Martin Nature Park Center.

Will Rogers Gardens is operated and maintained by the Botanical Gardens Division of the Parks and Recreation Department.

Stinchcomb Wildlife Refuge is managed by the Oklahoma City Water Trust.

The Oklahoma City Parks and Recreation Department cooperates with the Oklahoma City Water Utilities Trust in the permitting and management of recreational uses and activities at city reservoirs and surrounding lake reservations.

There are several guidelines to keep in mind when hiking Oklahoma City trails:

- Stay on designated trails.
- Weapons of any kind are prohibited.

- Fires are prohibited.
- Leave plants and animals undisturbed.
- Leash and pick up after your dogs.
- Do not litter.
- Glass bottles and containers are prohibited.
- Keep to the right of the path.
- Do not block trails; groups move to the right or form a single line.

For more information contact the Oklahoma City Parks and Recreation Department at (405) 297-3882 or visit www .okc.gov/trails.

Mitch Park is within the jurisdiction of the City of Edmond Parks and Recreation Department. For more information call (405) 359-4630 or visit http://edmondok .com/index.aspx?NID=337.

George Sutton Urban Wilderness Park is within the jurisdiction of the City of Norman Parks and Recreation Department. More information can be found by calling (405) 366-5472 or visiting www.normanok.gov/parks/ george-m-sutton-wilderness-park.

Oklahoma State Parks request that all visitors comply with their regulations to preserve and protect the natural resources within the parks. Oklahoma State Parks with trails covered in this book are Lake Thunderbird State Park, Red Rock Canyon State Park, and Roman Nose State Park.

Always follow state park regulations:

- Do not feed or catch wildlife.
- Do not collect nuts, berries, wildflowers, rocks, fossils, or any other type of natural item or species.

- Pets must be kept on a leash that is no more than 10 feet long.
- Do not leave pets unattended.
- Do not remove cultural or archaeological resources.
- Fireworks are prohibited.
- Keep the lakes and park litter- and pollution-free. Dispose of waste in the appropriate facilities provided for waste, sewage, and gray water.
- Glass containers and glass materials are not permitted in designated beach and swimming areas.
- Possessing or carrying a loaded weapon on one's person or in a motor vehicle is prohibited.
- Obscene actions, language, and behavior that disturb the peace are prohibited.
- Campfires must be contained in a fire ring—never leave a fire unattended.
- During dry periods, all campfires may be prohibited.

For a complete list of state park rules and policies, contact the individual state park office. More information can be found by referring to the Oklahoma Tourism and Recreation Department Travel Promotion Division website at www.travel ok.com/State_Parks. E-mail your requests to a staff member at information@TravelOK.com or call (800) 652-6552.

Safety and Preparation

There are several factors to consider when preparing for a hike in the metro Oklahoma City area. While all the hikes in this book are safe and easy, it is best to remember a few nuggets of advice should you find yourself in one of the following circumstances.

Weather Hazards

Remember that spring through midsummer has the most potential for rainstorms, flooding, and tornadoes. Always pack rain gear in your backpack. Being prepared and informed is your best defense. Seek shelter immediately during severe storms. Check your cell phone for updates or bring along a radio.

If you are outdoors when a tornado alert has been issued, take the following precautions:

- If near a building, get inside it immediately.
- If there is no shelter nearby, lie in a ditch or low-lying area, or crouch near a strong building. Be aware of the potential for flooding.
- Cover your head and neck with your arms while crouching down.
- Only in the most extreme conditions should you seek shelter under a highway overpass.

If you are outdoors during severe thunder and lightning activity, take the following precautions:

- Try to get into a car or a building.
- If you are in open space, squat low to the ground as quickly as possible. (If in the woods, find an area protected by a low clump of trees—never stand underneath a single large tree in the open.) Be aware of the potential for flooding in low-lying areas.
- Avoid tall structures and stay away from large bodies of water.
- Kneel or crouch with your hands on your knees.

For more information on tornado and thunderstorm/ lightning safety, refer to the State of Oklahoma government website at www.ok.gov/redirect.php?link_id=96.

Wildlife

The best way to prevent episodes with wildlife is to not disturb, feed, or approach the critters. Some wildlife species, like skunks and raccoons, can transmit rabies. Keep your pets on a leash to help prevent encounters. Even in city parks it is possible to see deer, armadillos, raccoons, and foxes. Be cautious while exploring the Wichita Mountains Wildlife Refuge as there are large populations of bison, elk, deer, and longhorn cattle roaming and grazing along trailheads and roads.

Ticks

You will find ticks in wooded areas, which include many of the trails within the state parks, refuge, and nature walks. Below are the Oklahoma State Department of Health's pre-cautions for preventing tick bites. Call (405) 271-4060 for more information on tick prevention precautions.

- Wear closed-toe shoes, not sandals.
- Wear light-colored clothing and long pants instead of shorts.
- Check for ticks along waistbands of clothing, the arm pits, and groin area during and after hiking.
- Use tick repellent according to directions.

Snakes

Stay on the trail and avoid bushwhacking around rocks and brush. Most snakes in Oklahoma are not poisonous. However, there are three that you should be aware of and know how to identify: copperhead, water moccasin, and rattlesnake. All snakebites should be immediately tended to by a medical professional. Head to the nearest hospital for evaluation and treatment. Contact the Oklahoma Poison Control Center at (800) 222-1222 for more information.

How to Use This Guide

This guide is designed to be simple and easy to use. The overview map at the beginning of the book shows the location of each hike by number, keyed to the table of contents. Each hike is accompanied by a route map that shows access roads, the highlighted featured route, and directional arrows to point you in the right direction. It indicates the general outline of the hike. Due to scale restrictions, it is not as detailed as a park map might be or even as our Miles and Directions are. Most of the hikes are very easy to navigate and provide options to add on or stop your hike early. You may want to visit the information or visitor's center of each location for additional resources and extra maps of the area.

Each hike begins with summary information that provides important trail statistics including length, difficulty, fees and permits, park hours, canine compatibility, and trail contacts. Directions to the trailhead are also provided, along with a general description of the natural and historic significance of each hike. A detailed route finder (Miles and Directions) sets forth mileages between significant landmarks along the trail.

Hike Selection

Hikes in this guide cover the northern, central, and southern Oklahoma City metro area from Edmond to Norman while including some spectacular hikes of state parks within an hour's drive or so from downtown Oklahoma City. All the trails are accessible to hikers of every age group and most are very easy and short. There are even opportunities to combine hikes with sight touring in the area, which you can find out more about by visiting TravelOK.com. Most of the hikes are less than 4 miles round-trip and are located along flat, well-managed trails that offer a variety of scenic and/or historic interest suitable for families, groups, or the solo hiker. However, there are a few hikes that offer some elevation and provide a more challenging trek in the state parks. The hikes are some of the best in the vast metro area from north to south and were selected for their accessible location and natural environment. They all offer a place to get away within the hubbub of the city. This guide serves as an introduction to the growing number of nature walks and hikes you can find in Oklahoma City.

Difficulty Ratings

Some might say the word "hiking" in Oklahoma City is a misnomer. The open space and city parks here are pretty tame. It's hard to get lost on these trails, and the level of difficulty really is more dependent on the weather than the technicality of the trails in this book. Locals have been "walking" neighborhood trails for years, but if you equate the word "hiking" with elevation gain along rugged mountain trails, it's pretty obvious that is not what you will get with the flatlands of Oklahoma City, with the exception of Roman Nose State Park, Red Rock Canyon State Park, and the Wichita Mountains Wildlife Refuge. Most of the hikes in this book are very easy with little climbing. They are, of course, completely subjective—consider that what you think is easy is entirely dependent on your level of fitness, review of the weather conditions, and the adequacy of your gear (primarily shoes). Remember to always be prepared and bring water no matter where you are going.

Approximate hiking times are based on the assumption that on flat ground most walkers average 2 miles per hour.

Adjust that rate by the steepness of the terrain and your level of fitness (subtract time if you're an aerobic animal and add time if you're hiking with kids), and you'll have a ballpark hiking duration. Be sure to add more time if you plan to picnic or take part in other activities like viewing wildlife or photography.

Trail Finder

Best Hikes for Wildlife Viewing
1. Martin Nature Park: A/B/C Trail
2. Martin Nature Park: Meadow Trail
18. Wichita Mountains Wildlife Refuge: Elk Mountain Trail
19. Wichita Mountains Wildlife Refuge: Longhorn Trail

Best Hikes for Nature Lovers and Birders
1. Martin Nature Park: A/B/C Trail
2. Martin Nature Park: Meadow Trail
6. Stinchcomb Wildlife Refuge: East Trail
7. Will Rogers Gardens Park

Best Hikes for History Lovers
11. Route 66 Park
12. Downtown Urban Museum Trail

Best Hikes for Children
1. Martin Nature Park: A/B/C Trail
16. Roman Nose State Park: Lake Dam Trail
17. Roman Nose State Park: Three Springs Trail

Best Hikes Near Lakes, Rivers, or Streams
4. Lake Hefner
6. Stinchcomb Wildlife Refuge: East Trail
13. Oklahoma River Trail: North
17. Roman Nose State Park: Three Springs Trail

Best Hikes for Geology Lovers

Best Hikes for Sunsets

Map Legend

════**44**════	Interstate Highway
───**81**───	US Highway
───**307**───	State Highway
───────	Local Road
= = = = = = =	Unpaved Road
├─┼─┼─┼─┤	Railroad
▬▬▬▬▬▬	Featured Trail
- - - - - - -	Trail
──────	Paved Trail
～～～	River/Creek
⬭	Body of Water
⬚⬚ ⬆	Local/State Park
➶	Boat Launch
⏝	Bridge
▲	Campground
✪	Capital
❷	Information Center
▲	Mountain/Peak
🅟	Parking
🛱	Picnic Area
■	Point of Interest/Trailhead
🚻	Restrooms
⌶	Tower
○	Town
⓫	Trailhead
⬕	Viewpoint/Overlook

1 Martin Nature Park: A/B/C Trail

A favorite outdoor family destination located in northwest Oklahoma City, this 144-acre nature park offers four easy trails through woods and meadows and over streams. The trails can be combined for one long hike if desired. There's also a hands-on educational facility where the knowledgeable staff presents special nature and wildlife programs that complement the seasons.

Distance: 1.5-mile circuit
Hiking time: About 1.5 hours
Difficulty: Easy, mostly flat with a few gentle uphills and steps
Trail surface: Gravel path and hard-packed dirt
Best season: Spring through fall
Other trail users: Schoolchildren on class field trips
Canine compatibility: Dogs not permitted
Fees and permits: None
Schedule: Wed to Sun from 9 a.m. to 6 p.m. Park is closed on all city holidays, as well as the week from Christmas Eve to New Year's Day.
Maps: Self-guided trail maps are available in the Educational Center; http://g.co/maps/m59p3
Trail contact: To speak to a Martin Nature Park Center naturalist, call the center at (405) 755-0676.
Other: A fee may be requested for special guided hikes. Call the office (405-755-0676) for a list of special guided hikes. Restrooms and water fountains are located inside the center.

Finding the trailhead: MNPC is located at 5000 W. Memorial Rd. in the far northwest corner of Oklahoma City. The nature park is set back from the south side of Memorial Road between MacArthur Boulevard and Meridian Avenue. To get there drive west along the John Kilpatrick Turnpike. Take the N. MacArthur Boulevard exit and go south to the first intersection which is W. Memorial Road. Turn east onto

W. Memorial Road. Drive just under a half mile and the entrance will be on your right. Turn into park. GPS: N35 36.411' / W97 36.550'

The Hike

This oasis of forested trails, streams, and tallgrass prairie meadows frequented by a variety of wildlife is a surprising habitat to explore since Martin Nature Park is flanked by busy roads and suburban developments. It's not what you would expect, which makes it seem like a small version of a state park thriving within the hubbub of city life. Totally enchanting, Martin Nature Park might even give you the sense that you have just visited Oklahoma City's version of Sherwood Forest.

From the parking lot there are two options for hiking. You can walk to the adjacent picnic pavilion and continue on the packed-earth path near it to hook up with the Meadow Trail. Or from the parking lot, you can walk directly to the signposts and follow the wide path toward the nature center, which will lead you to the signpost for Trail A, the start of this hike and also considered the gateway to Trails B and C. As you follow the path, there will be a bridge crossing. Look down at the water for floating turtles . . . if you can locate a spot past the clusters of wide-eyed young children peering transfixed at the wildlife below. Before you head out on Trail A, stop at the nature center located next to the trailhead. Stop and browse the small wildlife museum for examples of flora and fauna you might encounter in the park. Grab a free self-guided trail map that highlights key features to see along the way. Trail A leads to a bird-feeding station and onto the Observation Tower, where kids and adults can get a bird's-eye view of the canopy of trees in the park, including the state tree, the redbud. Trail B winds into the east end, where

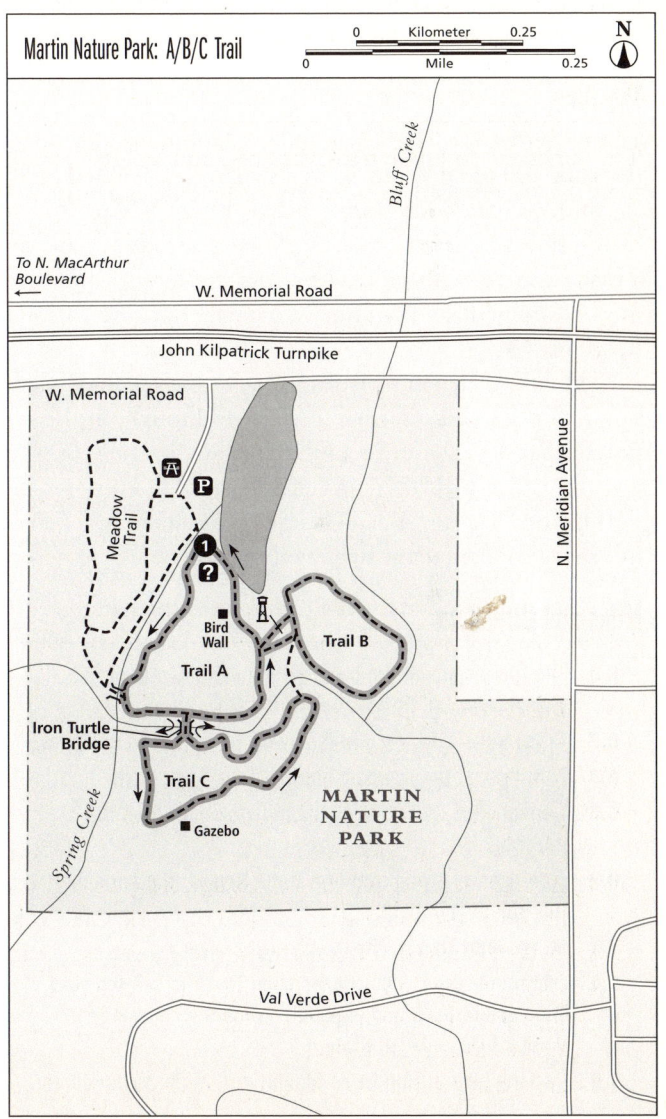

Martin Nature Park: A/B/C Trail

0 Kilometer 0.25
0 Mile 0.25

N

Bluff Creek

To N. MacArthur Boulevard

W. Memorial Road

John Kilpatrick Turnpike

W. Memorial Road

Meadow Trail

P

1

?

Bird Wall

Trail A

Trail B

Iron Turtle Bridge

Spring Creek

Trail C

Gazebo

MARTIN NATURE PARK

N. Meridian Avenue

Val Verde Drive

the well-marked trail winds toward Spring Creek and Bluff Creek. The wooded area opens up into a meadow, which is especially pretty when native wildflowers like orange-red Mexican hat are in bloom and fluttering butterflies and singing birds visit. Trail C meanders along the south side of the park and provides access to a small creek where families can observe creek life from a pebbled beach. Near the end of the trail is a gazebo that overlooks a meadow, providing a nice rest stop with great views of native grasses and wildflowers and perhaps a sighting of the state bird, the scissortail flycatcher.

The added benefits of this hike are the creative educational displays and informative signage throughout the trail system that describe the ecological habitat's variety of wildlife, and native natural environment typical in every season.

Option: Trails A, B, and C can all be hiked individually instead of in a circuit as suggested in this hike.

Miles and Directions

0.0 The trail begins at the back of the nature center at the Trail A signpost. Follow the gravel path.

0.2 Cross the service road and stay on Trail A, which veers left.

0.3 Turn right at the signpost onto Trail C.

0.5 Continue on Trail C. Enjoy the meadow view from the gazebo.

0.9 Turn right, crossing over Iron Turtle Bridge, and continue on the trail to your right.

1.1 Merge onto Trail B. (There is a sign marker.)

1.4 Climb the steps to the Observation Tower to see the view. Then climb down and continue on the trail, passing the Wildbird Observation Station.

1.5 End the hike at Honeybee Station next to the visitor center.

2 Martin Nature Park: Meadow Trail

The Meadow Trail is outside of the circuit hikes featured on the Martin Nature Park A/B/C Trail (Hike 1). This very brief hike is perfect as an add-on or great on its own. Families with babies or less mobile folks will find the flat path smooth and easygoing. Combine it with a picnic at the pavilion next to the trailhead and a visit to the nature center for a half-day outdoor excursion. The park is rehabilitating the meadow back to its original state of being filled with native tall prairie grasses.

Distance: 0.5-mile loop

Hiking time: About 20 minutes

Difficulty: Easy and flat

Trail surface: Hard-packed dirt and grass

Best season: Year-round

Other trail users: Schoolchildren on class field trips

Canine compatibility: Dogs not permitted

Fees and permits: None

Schedule: Wed to Sun from 9 a.m. to 6 p.m. Park is closed on all city holidays, as well as the week from Christmas Eve to New Year's Day.

Maps: Self-guided trail maps are available in the Educational Center. http://g.co/maps/m59p3

Trail contact: To speak to a Martin Nature Park Center naturalist, call the center at (405) 755-0676.

Other: A fee may be requested for special guided hikes. Call the office (405-755-0676) for a list of special guided hikes. Restrooms and water fountains are located inside the center. This hike can be combined with the Martin Nature Park: A/B/C Trail (Hike 1).

Finding the trailhead: MNPC is located at 5000 W. Memorial Rd. in the far northwest corner of Oklahoma City. The nature park is set back from the south side of Memorial Road between MacArthur

Boulevard and Meridian Avenue. To get there drive west along the John Kilpatrick Turnpike. Take the N. MacArthur Boulevard exit and go south to the first intersection which is W. Memorial Road. Turn east onto W. Memorial Road. Drive just under a half mile and the entrance will be on your right. Turn into park.

From the parking lot walk toward the picnic pavilion area. The trail begins on the edge of the picnic area. Look for the narrow strip of mowed grassy trail. GPS: N35 36.444' / W97 36.604'

The Hike

If you were a pioneer crossing the prairies in the nineteenth century, you would have encountered miles upon miles and wave upon wave of tall native prairie grass flowing like an ocean in middle America. Today there are few of these natural habitats left. Martin Nature Park replicates the grasslands of long ago in a small plot of land to provide visitors with a sense of Oklahoma's original habitat. The grass is literally "as high as an elephant's eye," as described in the Oklahoma state song from the musical *Oklahoma!*

Walk around the trail to see native plant life and wildlife that call the prairie home. Look up in the sky and you might see a hawk. Look on the ground for lizards or perhaps an armadillo. And if you are lucky, you might even see white-tailed deer foraging for a snack. Continue on around for glimpses of birdhouses and roosting boxes for local bird life.

From the start of the hike, you can go right or left and follow the trail until it leads back to the starting point. Enjoy the tallgrass meadow as you curve around the trail. At times the prairie grass can be as tall as an adult. Deer can be seen grazing at dawn and dusk. Look for horse apples along the grass near the trees.

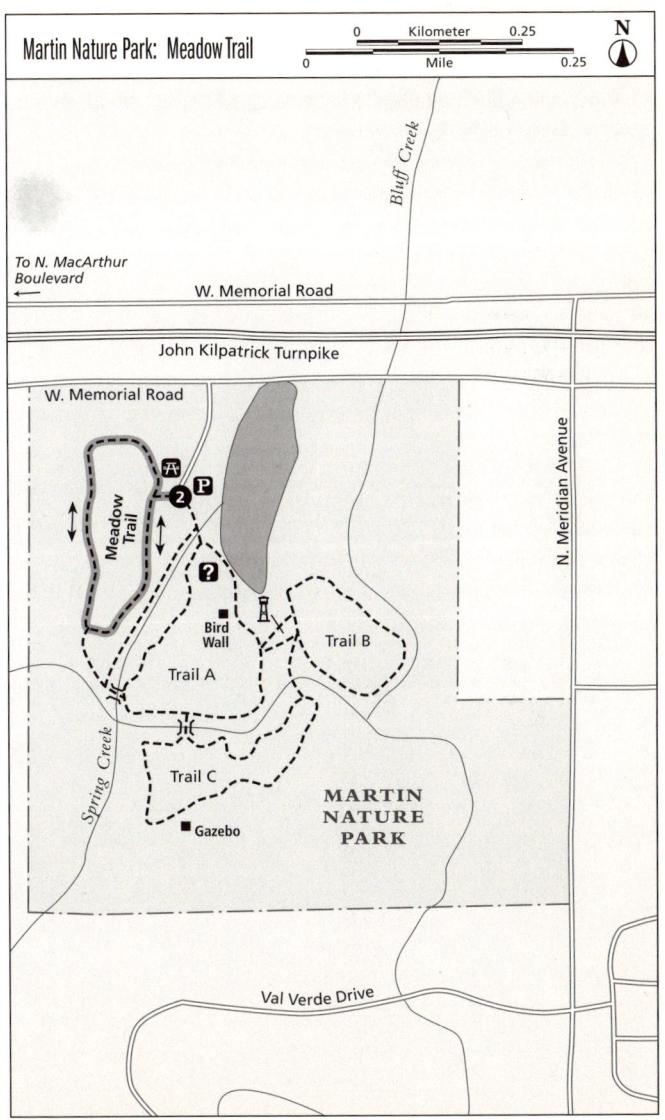

Martin Nature Park: Meadow Trail

0   Kilometer   0.25

0   Mile   0.25

N

To N. MacArthur Boulevard
←

W. Memorial Road

Bluff Creek

John Kilpatrick Turnpike

W. Memorial Road

Meadow Trail

2

P

?

N. Meridian Avenue

Bird Wall

Trail A

Trail B

Spring Creek

Trail C

Gazebo

MARTIN NATURE PARK

Val Verde Drive

Miles and Directions

0.0 The trail is a short loop. You may go left or right.

0.5 Follow the loop back to the starting point, the end of your hike.

3 Bluff Creek Trail

You will find this hidden gem slightly north of Lake Hefner. It's not the kind of trail you would expect near the developed parts of suburbia and that is what makes it so alluring. This small, forested, creek-side oasis with a packed-dirt single track awaits the hiker who enjoys "super eight" twisty turns, and lots of them, along with slight roller-coaster hills. Watch out for mountain bikers, especially on the turns, as this is one of the premier off-road trails in Oklahoma City for mountain biking.

Distance: 3.4-mile loop
Hiking time: About 2 hours
Difficulty: Easy with some rolling hills
Trail surface: Forested single track and dirt path
Best season: Spring through fall
Other trail users: Mountain bikers and trail runners
Canine compatibility: Leashed dogs permitted
Fees and permits: None
Schedule: Sunrise to sunset daily

Maps: http://okearthbike.com/trails.php
Facilities: Large parking area, trash cans, information board
Trail contact: Oklahoma Earth Bike Fellowship maintains the trail. E-mail oefwebguy@gmail.com.
Special considerations: Heavily used mountain-biking single-track trail. Trail may be closed after rain.
Other: Best time to go is during the week.

Finding the trailhead: The park is situated on the northwest corner of West Hefner Road and Meridian Avenue, approximately 1 mile west of Lake Hefner Parkway. Turn north onto Meridian Avenue from West Hefner Road. You will see the park sign and entrance from the road. Turn left into the Bluff Creek Park entrance and park in the lot. Walk to the trail sign indicating mountain bike trails. A few yards from the sign, you will see a narrow dirt trail with a trail marked ENTER. GPS: N35 35.018' / W97 36.370'

The Hike

Bluff Creek is a twister of a trail. Don't be daunted by all the turns and curves on the map. This trail is a lot of fun to hike largely due to very winding single- and double-track dirt paths. The path zigzags quite a bit so keep on the trail and follow the arrows indicating which way to go throughout the meadow and wooded areas. The trail is mostly hard-packed red dirt, but if it has been hot and dry for a while, the terrain could be sandy and dusty; after a good downpour prepare for a slick and muddy trail.

Keep your eyes on the path and your ears open because at any given moment, a mountain biker could be spinning toward you. Step aside to your right, to the edge of the trail, and let the biker pass you, then continue on your way. The cross-country, multiuse trail might reward you with a glimpse of wildlife, such as a hopping bunny in the woods or perhaps, depending on the time of day, you might even round a curve and see a whitetail deer foraging for food or taking a drink from the creek. Spiral your way through a maze of mature-growth trees, cross a number of wooden slat bridges with creek views, and hike up and down over a series of roller-coaster hills. Keep rambling through and before you know it, you will be at the end of the most surprising off-the-beaten-path trail in Oklahoma City.

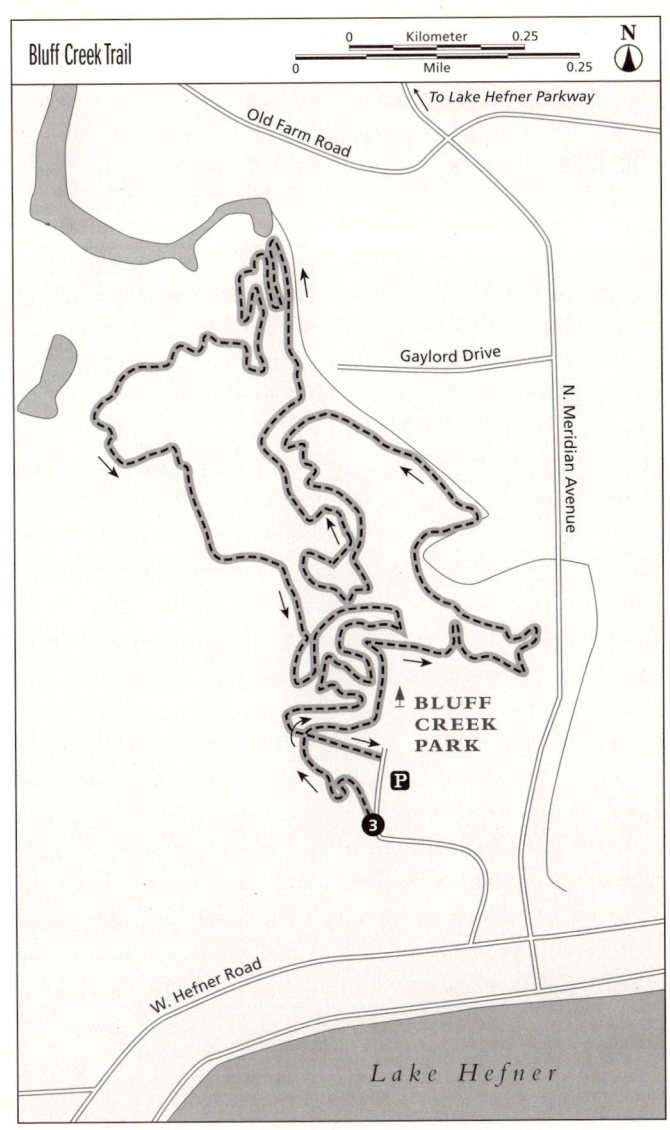

Bluff Creek Trail

0   Kilometer   0.25

0   Mile   0.25

N

Old Farm Road

To Lake Hefner Parkway

Gaylord Drive

N. Meridian Avenue

BLUFF
CREEK
PARK

P

3

W. Hefner Road

Lake Hefner

Miles and Directions

0.0 Begin the trail at the ENTER sign on the narrow dirt-packed path. Watch out for mountain bikers.

0.4 Cross the wide dirt path and continue on the single-track trail to your right. Throughout the hike the trail zigzags substantially. Keep on the trail and follow the arrow sign markers.

0.7 As you walk through a meadow, you will enter a wooded area through a beautiful natural cedar evergreen archway that frames the trail. Continue winding along the trail.

3.4 At the intersection in the trail, turn left and walk over the bridge onto the asphalt path, which leads back to the car and the end of the hike.

4 Lake Hefner

The most popular lakefront setting in Oklahoma City spans a circumference of about 10 miles. It's possible to walk the perimeter of the lake, but for a shorter hike head to the southern side, where a scenic stroll along the water's edge awaits near Lakeshore Park and Stars and Stripes Park. Here you can enjoy panoramic views of the lake and perhaps time it just right to see one of the many weekend sailboat races.

Distance: 3.7 miles out and back

Hiking time: About 2 hours

Difficulty: Easy due to flat, smooth terrain

Trail surface: Multipurpose asphalt trail

Best season: Year-round

Other trail users: Cyclists, in-line skaters, and joggers on designated sections of trail

Canine compatibility: Leashed dogs permitted

Fees and permits: None

Schedule: Open daily, sunrise to sunset year-round

Maps: www.okc.gov/trails/hefner.html

Trail contacts: E-mail randall.entz@okc.gov with the Oklahoma City government for more information on parks and trails, or call (405) 297-2211 to speak with a Parks and Recreation representative.

Other: Wheelchair accessible

Finding the trailhead: The expansive park is located between Lake Hefner Parkway and MacArthur Boulevard from Wilshire to NW 108th Street. Exit onto Britton Road toward the lake from the Lake Hefner Parkway (OK 74). Drive south on the service road toward the Children's Playground. Park in the lot. GPS: N35 33.578' / W97 34.655'

The Hike

The whole family will enjoy this hike as there are plenty of recreational options for all ages. Start off the hike from the Children's Playground parking lot and begin with some playtime if you have small ones with you. Kids can monkey around on the space-themed rocket-ship climbing structure or select from other distinctive playground equipment. The 12-foot-wide multiuse asphalt trail is just a few paces from the park and follows the shoreline toward Stars and Stripes Park, which is visible from the path with its prominent flagpole display of the extra-large American flag fluttering in the wind.

The location of the lake makes it a perfect venue to spot locals running, walking, or cycling along the path before or after work. Those are the busiest times so plan accordingly if you want more solitude on the trail. The trail hugs the shoreline so there are plenty of opportunities to see a variety of bird life, including heron, egrets, ducks, and geese perched along the banks and slender beaches, depending on the season. As you continue along the path, there is a small pond with an abundance of trees shading the trail. Look closely at the pond for snapping turtles perched on downed tree branches. There are plenty of excellent picnic areas with tables and benches dotting the lake's trail where hikers can rest and relax.

Lake Hefner is home to the Oklahoma City Boat Club so there is a good chance, from April to October, to observe sailboats plying the waters and perhaps catch sight of a race or regatta. The lake has docks and dry storage for boats as well as piers for fishing, but a permit is required to fish anywhere on the lake. Once you reach the Burt Cooper Loop,

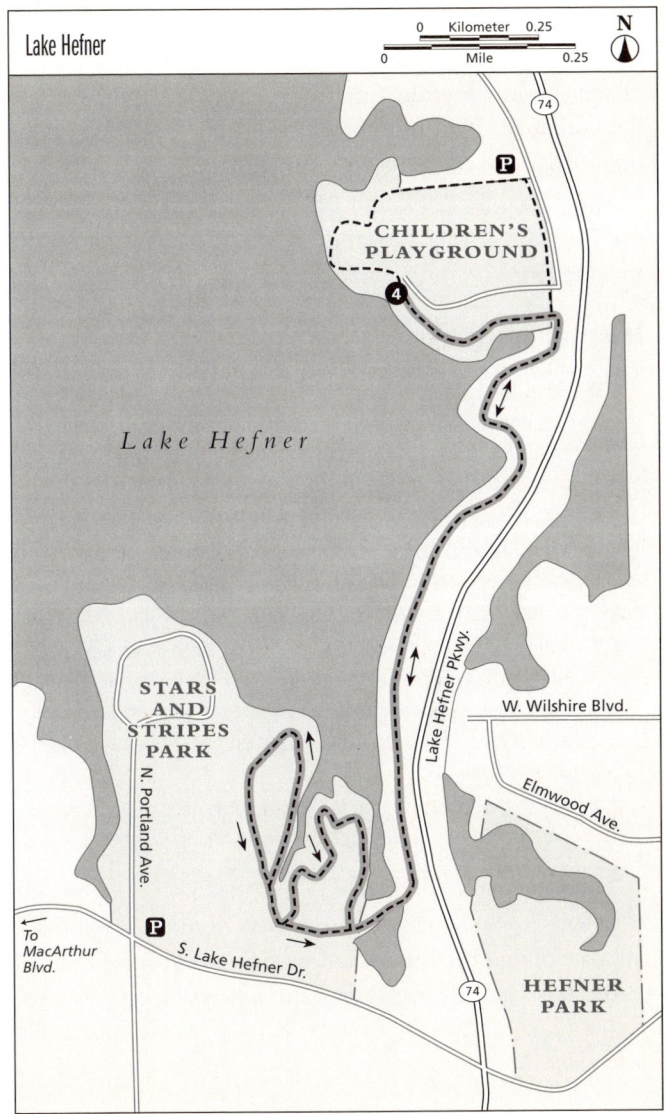

Lake Hefner

0   Kilometer   0.25

0   Mile   0.25

N

74

CHILDREN'S PLAYGROUND

P

4

Lake Hefner

Lake Hefner Pkwy.

STARS AND STRIPES PARK

N. Portland Ave.

W. Wilshire Blvd.

Elmwood Ave.

P

To MacArthur Blvd.

S. Lake Hefner Dr.

74

HEFNER PARK

you can follow that very brief section, continue on to Stars and Stripes Park, or double-back on the trail and return to the Children's Playground parking lot.

Lake Hefner offers a beautiful setting for sunset watching, especially from this location, where hikers are rewarded with birds soaring in a colorful changing sky and sailboats moving placidly across the lake while the sun drops below the horizon. This is a stunning sunset shoreline hike that is most unexpected in a landlocked state.

Miles and Directions

0.0 Start the hike from the Children's Playground parking lot. Walk toward the asphalt hiking trail on the south side. The trail hugs the lakeshore, curving toward Stars and Stripes Park further south.

1.6 You have the option to go left, right, or straight. Turn right onto the trail. Continue on the trail as it hugs and loops close to the lake. This part of trail is sheltered with a canopy of trees, with some nice spots to rest on park benches.

1.7 After finishing the short loop, you wind onto the main pedestrian path. Notice the LAKE HEFNER TRAILS sign. Veer right onto the pedestrians-only path to the Burt Cooper Loop. You will see the sign honoring Burt Cooper on your right as you continue on the path.

2.3 Finish the loop and turn left at the intersection. Double-back along the path back to the Children's Playground.

3.7 End the hike back at the Children's Playground.

5 Dolese Youth Park

Located in the middle of central Oklahoma City, the 139-acre multipurpose youth park is complete with walk/run/bike trails, baseball fields, a fishing pond, playground equipment, and a disc golf course. The hard-packed dirt trail circling the park was paved in early 2012, according to Oklahoma City Parks and Recreation.

Distance: 2.1-mile loop
Hiking time: About 1 hour
Difficulty: Easy and flat
Trail surface: Paved and Hard-packed dirt
Best season: Year-round
Other trail users: Joggers and cyclists
Canine compatibility: Leashed dogs permitted

Fees and permits: None
Schedule: 5 a.m. to 11 p.m. daily
Maps: Contact Parks and Recreation office of City of Oklahoma City at (405) 297-2211
Trail contacts: Parks and Recreation office of City of Oklahoma City, 420 W. Main, Oklahoma City, OK 73102, (405) 297-2211

Finding the trailhead: Located 1 block west of NW 50th Street and Meridian. Go south on Lake Hefner Parkway and exit onto NW 50th. Follow NW 50th west for about 1.25 miles, turn right into the park's main entrance and drive to back parking lot. Entrance is directly south of Putnam City High School. GPS: N35 30.330' / W97 34.776'

The Hike

Once a gravel pit, the Dolese Youth Park is now a well-used, well-maintained neighborhood park situated directly across from Putnam City High School. Walk the perimeter of the

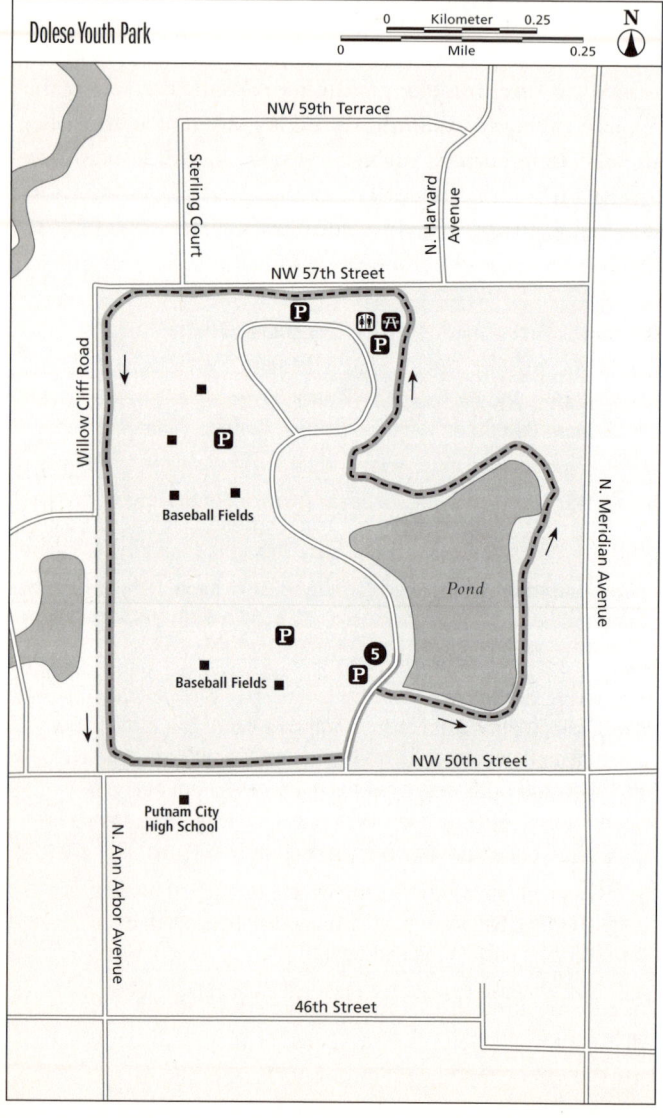

Dolese Youth Park

0   Kilometer   0.25
0   Mile   0.25

N

NW 59th Terrace

Sterling Court

N. Harvard Avenue

NW 57th Street

Willow Cliff Road

Baseball Fields

Baseball Fields

Pond

N. Meridian Avenue

NW 50th Street

N. Ann Arbor Avenue

Putnam City High School

46th Street

nature trail and you might even hear the school band practicing out on the fields—the park is that close to the high school. Football game nights in the fall might be some of the more festive evenings for a meander around the trail. But if you are looking for solitude, try hiking the trail at an earlier time or a different day.

The park is a great option for those looking for an outdoor natural area in the middle of residential Oklahoma City. It offers an easy trail for getting a quick hike in during the day.

Follow the trail as it hugs the pond for a view of geese and ducks. You might even encounter fishermen along the way. As you follow the path, it will curve and straighten out to parallel residential NW 57th Street. Spurs off the main path lead to playground areas, the picnic shelter, and the school fields. Continue on past forested parts of the park. The trail will curve left, looping back to the starting point. You will see the soccer field to your left and the high school in front of you. Continue on to the parking lot.

Miles and Directions

0.0 From the parking lot walk toward the small pond and follow the path around it.

1.1 There are several spurs off of the main path that lead to playground areas or a picnic shelter, and another parking area is located here.

1.7 The path opens up to a soccer field to your left and Putnam City High School in front of you. Continue along the path, winding back to the parking lot.

2.1 End the hike back at the main entrance parking lot.

6 Stinchcomb Wildlife Refuge: East Trail

The natural environment of the refuge is considered one of the best-kept secrets in the city. The main hiking trail is a fairly straight dirt path that connects with four small ponds leading to the North Canadian River. Birders will enjoy spotting a variety of species.

Distance: 5.2 miles out and back

Hiking time: About 2.5 hours

Difficulty: Easy and flat

Trail surface: Hard-packed dirt path

Best season: Year-round

Other trail users: Mountain bikers, ATVs, joggers

Canine compatibility: Leashed dogs permitted

Fees and permits: None

Schedule: Daily; dawn to dusk

Maps: Stinchcomb Wildlife Refuge is managed by the Oklahoma City Water Trust, (405) 297-1525

Trail contact: Parks and Recreation office of City of Oklahoma City, 420 W Main, Oklahoma City, OK 73102, (405) 297-2211

Special considerations: Watch for poison ivy along the sides of the trail.

Other: Another trail suitable for hiking is found on the west side of the refuge at the intersection of County Line and Morgan Roads.

Finding the trailhead: The refuge lies just north of Lake Overholser (north of US 66/AKA NW 39th Expwy.). Follow NW 39th Expressway east and turn north on Council Road. After 0.75 mile, turn west onto NW 50th. Turn right onto N. Stinchcomb Road. The main hiking trail can be accessed on the east side of the refuge at NW 51st and N. Stinchcomb Road, just north of 50th and west of Council Road. GPS: N35 31.402' / W97 39.819'

The Hike

The hard-packed dirt path of the East Trail offers a wide and flat route, which is shared with mountain bikers, joggers, and ATVs. So listen carefully for other users along the trail as not everyone practices good trail-sharing etiquette. Weekends tend to be the busiest. This is one of the longest hikes in the book but quite flat and easy. Bring water and snacks for a nice break.

This easy out-and-back is best for morning or late afternoon hikes for a chance to see wildlife and to keep out of the heat of midday sun. You might come across the pronged hoof marks of deer tracks along the trail or hear the rummaging of an armadillo near the path as it rustles through the leaves. At times the refuge is marshy in places and it is thickly wooded. Keep a look out for poison ivy on the edges of the trail. A good rule of thumb to identify the culprit is "leaves of three, let it be." You will spot pecan trees on either side of the trail. Search for the lime-colored outer casing along the sides of the trail. The casing is the size a golf ball and houses the nut inside. You will also see plenty of the infamous and intrusive red cedar trees lining the path.

Look up into the canopy of trees to glimpse birdlife. The Oklahoma City Audubon Society recommends the Stinchcomb Wildlife Refuge as a great viewing spot for birders. During any season you might be accompanied by birdsong along the route and might even catch a glimpse of the scissortail flycatcher, the Oklahoma state bird. Depending on the season, expect to see Mississippi kites, red-tailed hawks, and great horned, barred, and eastern screech owls. Small birds are trickier to see but look for Carolina wrens, woodpeckers, American goldfinches, and indigo buntings.

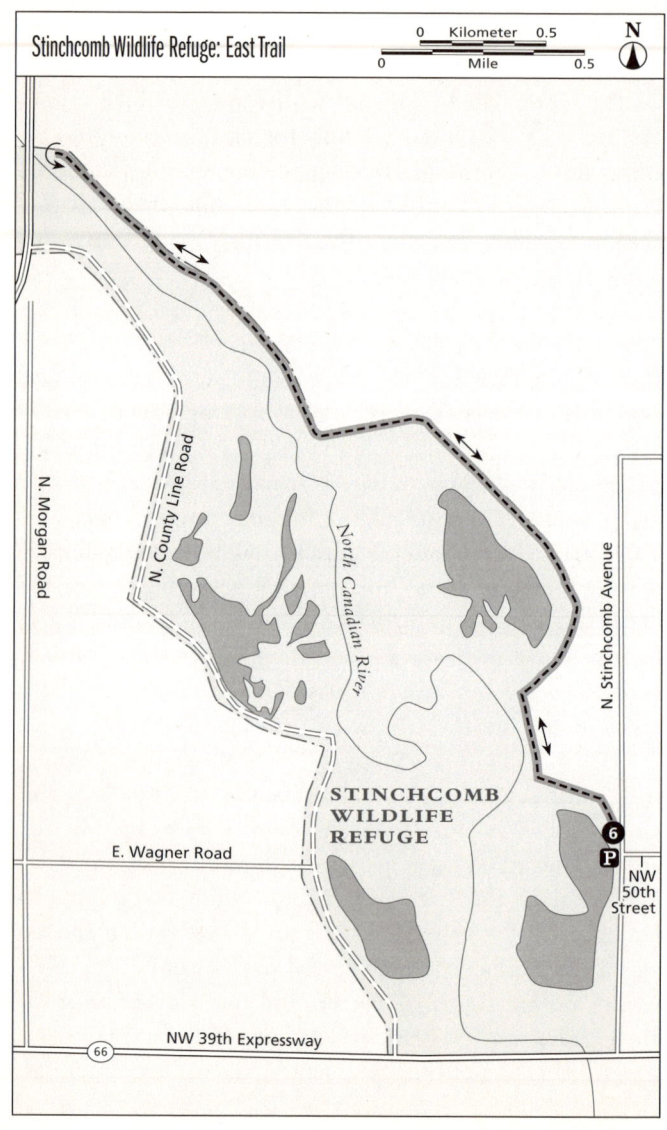

Stinchcomb Wildlife Refuge: East Trail

0   Kilometer   0.5
0   Mile   0.5

N

N. Morgan Road

N. County Line Road

North Canadian River

N. Stinchcomb Avenue

STINCHCOMB
WILDLIFE
REFUGE

E. Wagner Road

6
P
NW
50th
Street

66   NW 39th Expressway

Near the ponds or small lakes, look for wood ducks and warblers. During migration periods in spring and fall, bring binoculars to view a variety of birds in abundance.

The refuge is also popular with canoeists and kayakers due to its easy access to the North Canadian River, which becomes the Oklahoma River as it flows through downtown Oklahoma City. The end of the trail is at the junction of the North Canadian River, where you will double-back on the trail. There is another trail on the west side of the river, however, the East Trail is considered the main trail.

Miles and Directions

0.0 Walk toward the trailhead from the parking lot. The wide packed-dirt trail begins just past the red, white, and blue gate.

2.6 The trail is fairly straight all the way to the junction with the North Canadian River. At this point turn around and double-back toward the beginning of the trailhead.

5.2 Reach the end of the trail.

7 Will Rogers Gardens Park

Will Rogers Gardens spread across 30 acres of one of the most historic parks in Oklahoma City. The park features the Charles E. Sparks Rose Garden, which blooms from April through October, and the Margaret Annis Boys Arboretum, offering trails that wind around an impressive variety of 15 acres of trees and shrubs, including Oklahoma native species and specimens rarely found in the state. There is also the Ed Lycan Conservatory, home to the largest cacti and succulent collection in Oklahoma, and the Will Rogers Garden Exhibition Center. Pick up a self-guided tour map that provides more detail of all the garden species. You can find it at the Garden Exhibition building.

Distance: 0.9-mile loop
Hiking time: About 1 hour
Difficulty: Easy and flat
Trail surface: Asphalt and nature trail
Best season: Apr through Oct
Other trail users: Joggers
Canine compatibility: Leashed dogs permitted
Fees and permits: None
Schedule: Open daily; year-round dawn to dusk
Maps: A free Horticultural Gardens and Arboretum self-guided tour map is available in the Will Rogers Gardens Exhibition Building, located at 3400 NW 36th St. Contact Parks and Recreation office of City of Oklahoma City at (405) 297-2211. The Will Rogers Gardens are operated and maintained by the Botanical Gardens Division of the Parks and Recreation Department.
Trail contacts: Will Rogers Gardens Exhibition Center, 3400 NW 36th St., (405) 943-0827.
Other: Free garden tours are available upon advanced request. Contact staff at the Garden Exhibition building for information or to make a reservation at (405) 943-0827.

Finding the trailhead: The vast Will Rogers Park system is centered between N. Portland Avenue and N. Grand Boulevard and NW 36th and NW 30th Streets. There are several entrances into the park. For this hike within Will Rogers Gardens, it is best to drive along the N. Grand Boulevard (parallel to I-44) side of the park and turn onto Pat Murphy Drive. Follow Pat Murphy Drive until you reach the Senior Citizens Building parking lot. From the parking lot walk to the iron-gated main entrance to Will Rogers Gardens. GPS: N35 30.330' / W97 34.776'

The Hike

The gardens are part of the larger Will Rogers Park system and provide a nice restorative getaway from the hustle and bustle of the daily grind. Their central location makes the gardens a favorite with locals for a quick break. Access this hike via the Senior Citizens Center parking lot and enter through the iron gate. At this point you have a choice to either turn right and cross a bridge to begin at the Rose Garden or to continue straight and follow the flat gravel dirt path leading to the arboretum, the route for this hike. The arboretum is adjacent to two small lakes, and you can enjoy the shaded canopy of hundreds of species of trees here as you loop around the trail.

Discover native species like the magnificent umbrella magnolia tree that blooms with creamy white flowers from May to early June. Walk by stands of maples, especially pretty in fall with blazing displays of yellow to orange to red leaves. Wander through the groves of oaks, Chinese junipers, eastern red cedars, crab apple trees, pines, redbuds, and lots of shrubs. Those with green thumbs will appreciate the variety and careful maintenance of the gardens and trees. As you approach the Pear Grove, veer right onto the trail, which leads to the Rose Garden and other park features.

This short hike can easily occupy a few hours' time enjoying the beauty of the many flowers in bloom, including daylilies, peonies, irises, azaleas, and other plants. The real showstopper of the vibrant flora is the formal rose garden, with eighty-five varieties of roses on more than 800 individual rose bushes. You will wind around the formal gardens and catch sight of a charming little Hobbit-like bridge that crosses a trickling stream. Follow the trail or take off on one of the short spurs near the water for a nice place to rest. Enjoy the garden pathways and listen for the cicadas chirping, or watch for butterflies fluttering around the bright blooms.

The best time to see an abundance of roses in bloom is mid-May and September through October. Look for the sculpted bust of Will Rogers, the famous nineteenth-century Oklahoma humorist, perched in a private nook north of the iris specialty garden. In the middle of the Rose Garden, you will see the other famous statue, a lovely bronze that depicts a mother and daughter. Follow the sidewalk leading to the larger bridge near the entry—you will likely see a few ducks splashing around in the pond nearby. Cross the bridge and continue back to the start of the trail to complete the hike.

Miles and Directions

0.0 Walk through the iron gate and follow the dirt and gravel path to your left.

0.2 You will see a pond to your right with a squadron of ducks and geese patrolling the shoreline. You will see tennis courts as you continue walking the nature path.

0.4 Continue following the path around the perimeter of the arboretum, viewing the vast collection of trees. As you come

Will Rogers Gardens Park

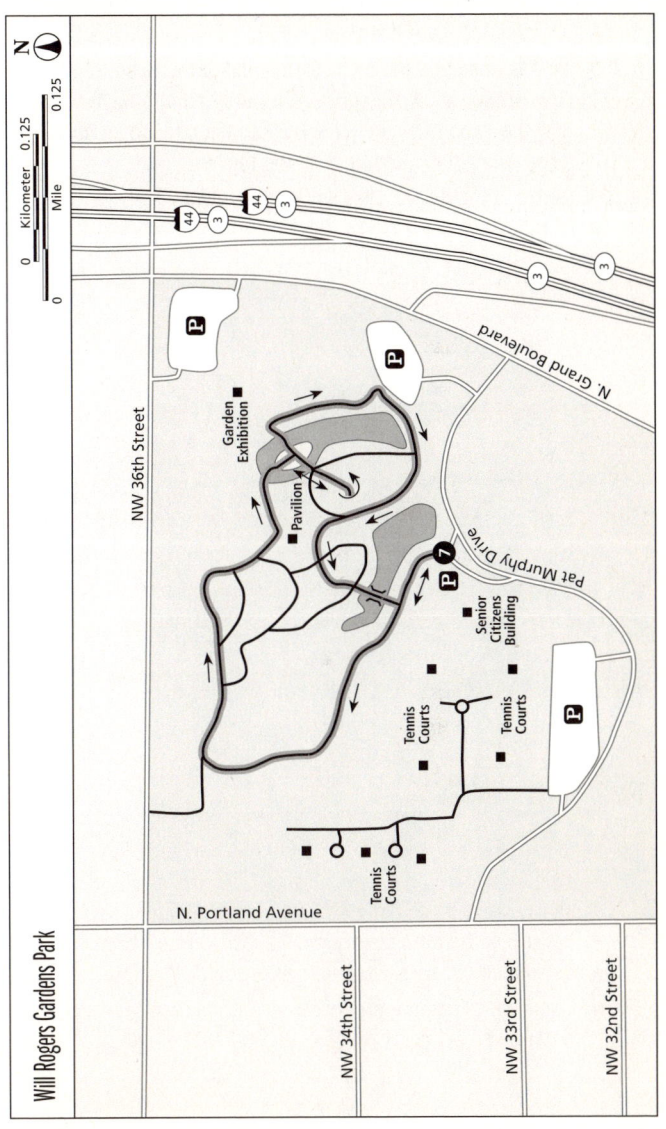

N

0 Kilometer 0.125
0 Mile 0.125

NW 36th Street

Garden Exhibition

Pavilion

N. Grand Boulevard

Pat Murphy Drive

P

P

P 7

Senior Citizens Building

Tennis Courts

Tennis Courts

Tennis Courts

N. Portland Avenue

NW 34th Street

NW 33rd Street

NW 32nd Street

44 3

44 3

3

3

to the Pear Grove, veer right. This path leads to the Rose Garden and water features.

0.5 At this point you will be in the middle of the Rose Garden. You will see a bronze statue of a mother and daughter. Follow the route of your choice back to the parking lot, or continue along this route back to the trailhead.

0.9 Arrive at the Senior Citizens Center parking lot.

8 Mitch Park

A city park in Edmond, Mitch Park is a large, multiuse recreational park venue. Its location within the residential area of Edmond in northern Oklahoma City makes it ideal for family visits after work or on weekends. On any given day you can expect to see walkers and joggers along the asphalt path that frames the park exterior.

Distance: 2.7-mile loop
Hiking time: About 1.3 hours
Difficulty: Easy
Trail surface: Paved path
Best season: Year-round
Other trail users: Joggers
Canine compatibility: Leashed dogs permitted
Fees and permits: None
Schedule: Dawn to dusk
Maps: Edmond Parks and Recreation Office, (405) 359-4630.

Visit in person at the Multi Activity Center located at the west entrance to Mitch Park on Covell between Kelly and Santa Fe Avenues. Go online for a park map at http://edmondok.com/Facilities.aspx?Page=detail&RID=19.
Trail contacts: 1501 W. Covell Road, (405) 359-4630

Finding the trailhead: The park is located between N. Santa Fe Avenue and N. Kelly Avenue, with the entrance on W. Covell Road. Cheyenne Middle School borders the park near N. Kelly Avenue. Driving north on Kelly Avenue from Oklahoma City, turn left at W. Covell Road. You will see the large 280-acre park on your right. Turn right into the main entrance at Kiowa Drive. Park in the Senior Center parking lot. GPS: N35 40.960' / W97 30.436'

The Hike

Mitch Park is located at the very northern portion of metro Oklahoma City within the north end of Edmond. The multiuse park was named in honor of one of Edmond's foremost citizens of the nineteenth century, John Lewis Mitch, who was quite active in establishing community development during the town's early years of the 1890s. As the largest city park in Edmond, the 280-acre venue receives plenty of visitors both young and old who enjoy a plethora of recreational options. The paved trail borders the park, allowing you to view all the other active choices to fill up a day before or after a hike.

The paved main trail is accessible from a number of parking lots within the park. This hike begins across from the parking lot of the Senior Center. For the most part the trail is "pancake flat," however, there are a few small rolling hills along an occasional bridge crossing of small creeks and ditches. Wooded areas offer nice shade in the summer months with patches of tree canopy interspersed throughout the perimeter of the park. Occasionally you will come across a bench for a break if needed. This is a point where you can reflect on the plains and prairies of yesteryear as Edmond is centered at the intersection where the tallgrass prairies wove their way like a great wave blending with the woodlands and forest vegetation known as the Cross Timbers. This subregion where the plains and the prairies met was called the Osage Plains. What you will see today are flatlands of the park, with its many attractions bordered by major roads and Cheyenne Middle School.

Friendly locals walk or jog the main paved trail and the additional 1.8 miles of inner trails at any point during the

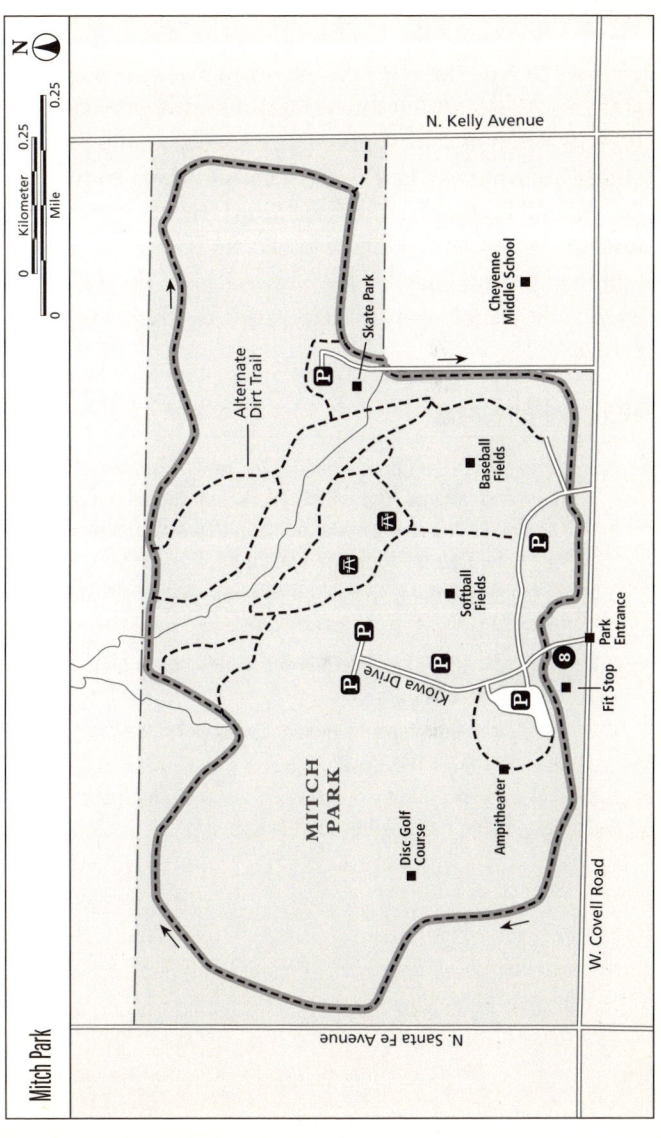

Mitch Park

N

0   Kilometer   0.25

0   Mile   0.25

N. Kelly Avenue

Cheyenne Middle School

Skate Park

Alternate Dirt Trail

Baseball Fields

Softball Fields

MITCH PARK

Kiowa Drive

Disc Golf Course

Ampitheater

Fit Stop

Park Entrance

N. Santa Fe Avenue

W. Covell Road

day. During softball and baseball season, depending on the time of day, you might hear the crack of a bat or the roar of a crowd as fans cheer on their favorite team in the fields as you pass by. Be sure to catch the skateboarders at the Skate Park as kids pull some stunning tricks that might even stop you in your tracks. There is also a basketball court, volleyball court, and my favorite, the Fit Stop, which offers a great way to extend your exercise time outdoors with parkland gym equipment. There's a leg press machine, EasyRider, and even a set of multi-bars to help you with stretching pre- or post-hike.

Miles and Directions

0.0 From the Senior Citizens parking lot, walk south toward the main asphalt trail. You will cross a small wooden bridge. Continue a few feet toward the main trail and turn right to begin the hike following the main path.

1.2 At the fork in the trail, turn left to continue with the main trail.

2.0 Veer right at the fork. You will see a park bench off the trail for a shady resting spot.

2.2 Turn left at the triangle junction. Continue on the main path back to the starting point.

2.7 End your hike and try out the exercise equipment at the Fit Stop before heading back to the car.

9 Lake Thunderbird: Hog Creek Trail

Lake Thunderbird is a frequent destination for Norman locals looking to cool off during the hot summer months. Hog Creek Trail is conveniently located near Zoom Beach for splashing about before or after the woodsy hike.

Distance: 2.4 miles out and back
Hiking time: About 1 hour, 10 minutes
Difficulty: Easy and slightly rolling
Trail surface: Hard-packed dirt
Best seasons: Spring and fall
Other trail users: Runners
Canine compatibility: Leashed dogs permitted
Fees and permits: None
Schedule: The park is open for camping and recreation 24 hours a day, 365 days a year.

Maps: http://okiedoke.com/LALedger/hogcreektrail.jpg, www.travelok.com
Trail Contact: The park office is at 13101 Alameda Dr., Norman, OK 73026, (405) 360-3572.
Other: The park offers 11 picnic shelters for groups, which may be reserved through the park office. Accommodations include more than 200 RV sites with 30 full-hookup sites, restroom facilities, and primitive campsites.

Finding the trailhead: The Indian Point side of Lake Thunderbird is located 9.0 miles east of Norman on Alameda Drive. The park can be accessed from downtown Norman by driving along Alameda Drive east all the way until reaching the Indian Point entrance. Continue on Alameda Drive until you reach a stop sign in the park indicating Little Sandy area. Turn left at sign for Little Sandy. Continue to parking lot near Zoom Beach and Hog Creek Camp. There are a few options for entry into the park. Call the park office for directions at (405) 360-3572. GPS: N35 14.792' / W97 14.362'

The Hike

The 1,874 acres of land stretching across the park wraps around a 6,000-acre man-made reservoir perched in Norman, Oklahoma. The lake is also considered the largest body of water within a 100-mile radius. The park features two marinas, Calypso Cove Marina and Little River Marina, nine boat ramps, and a swim beach. When visitors aren't in the water swimming, skiing, or boating, they take to the hiking and nature trails that lead through rolling, oak-covered hills and sandy shores surrounding the lake. Even country-western singer and native Oklahoman Toby Keith has fond memories of growing up near the lake, which inspired his song "Kissin' in the Rain."

Although there are more multiuse trails to explore on the Clear Bay side of Lake Thunderbird, the Hog Creek Trail is easy to access and is close to Indian Point Information Center on Alameda Drive, the main road from the town of Norman into the park. It's also a bit more quiet and tucked away.

At the very beginning of the out-and-back trail, there is a wildlife trail sign that indicates types of common mammals you might see along the trail including whitetail deer, beaver, raccoon, bobcat, striped skunk, and the "federation" ground squirrel—known for the stars-and-stripes pattern of its coat. Follow the narrow red dirt trail. Either side has a canopy of mature oak trees that provide shade. At any time of the year, you may rustle through a carpet of fallen oak leaves on the trail. Spring, summer, and fall are the best seasons to wander along the short, rolling trail, with highlights to be seen each season.

The scissortail flycatcher, the state bird, is known to enjoy this area. Perhaps you will see one in flight, ready

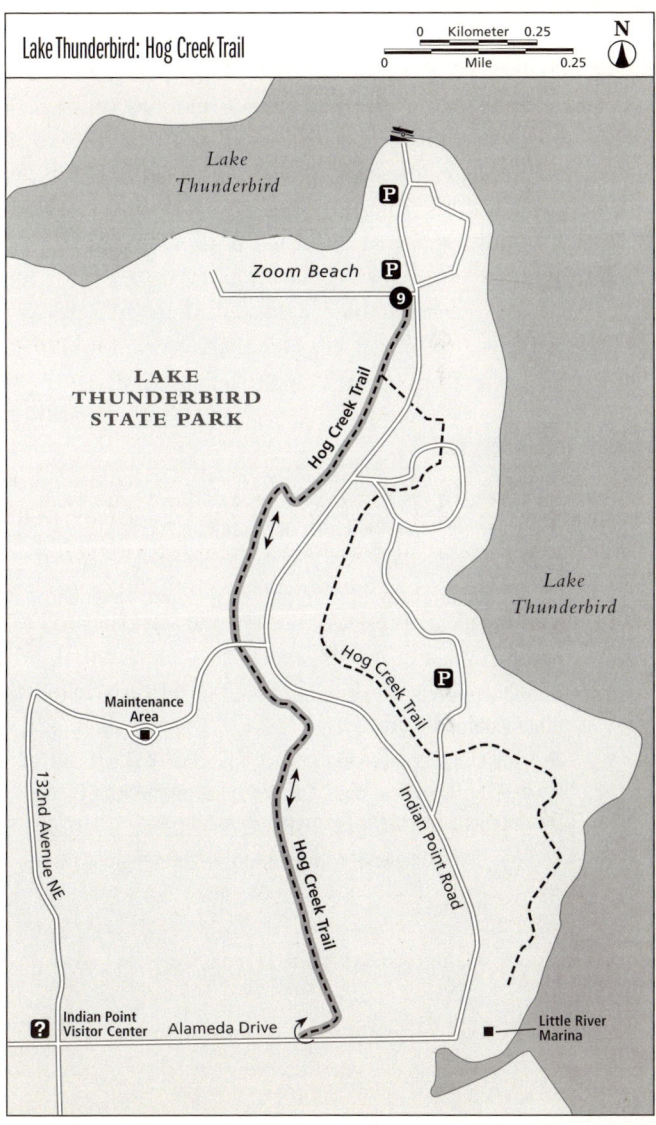

Lake Thunderbird: Hog Creek Trail

Kilometer 0.25

Mile 0.25

N

Lake Thunderbird

Zoom Beach

9

LAKE THUNDERBIRD STATE PARK

Hog Creek Trail

Hog Creek Trail

Lake Thunderbird

Maintenance Area

Hog Creek Trail

Indian Point Road

132nd Avenue NE

Hog Creek Trail

Indian Point Visitor Center

Alameda Drive

Little River Marina

to snag a snack of high-flying insects. A number of birds and butterflies flit about the treetops and grassy meadows near the lake. Ask park rangers for a list for your reference. As you wander along the path, enjoy nature's umbrella of trees overhead, from red cedar to pine and oak trees to the smaller scrublike trees and native grasses. This is a nice hike for relaxing and restoring the senses while breathing in the scent of woods, especially the dried pine needles crunching underfoot.

Once you reach the end of the trail that intersects with Alameda Drive, you might enjoy the chance to double-back and revel again along nature's aromatherapy trail.

Miles and Directions

0.0 The trail starts near the Zoom Beach sign. There is a wildlife trail sign indicating the types of mammals you might see while hiking the trail. Start the trail at this point.

0.4 Cross a small wooden bridge over a creek and continue on the path, where you will be shaded by a variety of tree canopy.

0.6 A road intersects the path. Continue along the path at the other side of the road.

1.2 The trail stops at the main paved park road. You will see an Indian Point Hiking Trail sign. Double-back on the Hog Creek Trail at this point for the remainder of the hike.

2.4 End the hike back where you started, at the trailhead.

10 George Sutton Urban Wilderness Park

Considered a little wilderness oasis within a small-town suburban environment, the park boasts 160 acres within a wooded natural environment far enough away from the sound of cars on busy city streets to make you feel like you are in the country. The park is located in the town of Norman, which is a quick thirty-minute drive south from downtown Oklahoma City and is home to the University of Oklahoma (OU).

Distance: 2.5-mile circuit
Hiking time: About 2 hours
Difficulty: Easy
Trail surface: Hard-packed red-dirt path
Best seasons: Spring and fall
Other trail users: Joggers
Canine compatibility: Leashed dogs permitted
Fees and permits: None
Schedule: Dawn to dusk

Maps: Managed by Norman Parks and Recreation, (405) 366-5472; www.normanok.gov/parks/george-m-sutton-wilderness-park
Trail Contact: Norman Parks and Recreation, 201-C West Gray, Norman, OK 73070; (405) 366-5472, www.normanok.gov/parks/george-m-sutton-wilderness-park

Finding the trailhead: Norman is approximately 25 miles south of Oklahoma City. Drive south on I-35 from the Oklahoma City metro area and take exit 110B towards Robinson Street. Turn slight right at about 0.16 mile onto W. Robinson Street and continue straight for about 3 miles and it becomes E. Robinson Street. Follow E. Robinson until you reach 12th Avenue Northeast (US 77), then turn south at the intersection. Drive straight for 2.5 miles until you reach the park entrance on your right. Park in the lot. GPS: N35 14.547' / W97 25.460'

The Hike

This peaceful park is a nice place to explore. A small web of trails takes you through many examples of native Oklahoma habitat including a few small lakes. The fields of the park have been planted with native grasses and are bordered with evergreens and other plantings.

There is good reason why the park was named after the well-respected local ornithologist George Miksch Sutton. Spring bird migration to the area brings numerous species to the park, including warblers, late wintering sparrows, and painted buntings as well as a variety of nesting birds. In the height of the spring months, you could be sharing the trail with Audubon hiking members.

You will follow the main trail at the gazebo from the parking lot entrance. There are plenty of spurs off the main trail that can take you to other park features such as the Frisbee golf course or perhaps a scenic lake vista. These trails wind through the trees, where you might encounter deer tracks and possibly discover beaver dams along the lake. As you follow the trail, listen for the loud buzz of cicadas during the summer months. Along the ground look for "horse apples," as they are known by the locals. The round sphere resembles an exotic Asian fruit with a pebbly lime-green exterior about the size of a baseball. Horses like to eat them, thus the name.

The trail connects to one of the small lakes. Spend a few minutes enjoying the beach, combing the shoreline for little shells. Then wind back to the main trail, where you will continue back to the starting point to end the hike.

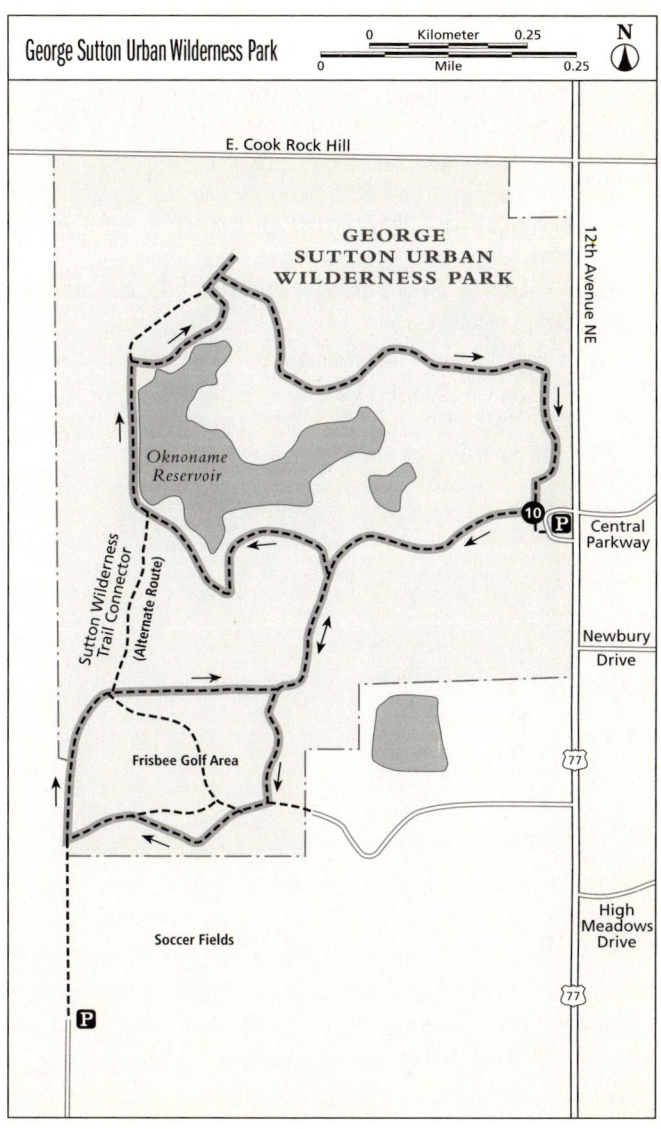

George Sutton Urban Wilderness Park

Kilometer 0.25

Mile 0.25

N

E. Cook Rock Hill

GEORGE
SUTTON URBAN
WILDERNESS PARK

12th Avenue NE

Oknoname
Reservoir

10 P Central
Parkway

Sutton Wilderness Trail Connector
(Alternate Route)

Newbury
Drive

77

Frisbee Golf Area

High
Meadows
Drive

77

Soccer Fields

P

Miles and Directions

0.0 Begin at gazebo trail marker, following the main Sutton trail. There are a number of spurs off the main trail that lead to different features in the park including a Frisbee golf course and a lake.

1.3 Wind along the trail within the Frisbee golf course area as it curves back to the main trail. Then continue on the main trail.

1.6 Continue on the trail to observe the lake, then veer left as it wraps around the lake.

2.0 Follow the path in the meadow as it connects to the main trail, where you will double-back along the main trail to the starting point.

2.5 End the hike back at the gazebo and parking lot area.

11 Route 66 Park

The newest jewel of the Oklahoma City Parks and Recreation Department, Route 66 Park bumps up within a few hundred yards of Lake Overholser in south-central Oklahoma City. The park was named after legendary Route 66, which runs parallel to the park where the historic Mother Road's route led from Chicago through Oklahoma City to Santa Monica. Visitors will see a decorative and artistically stamped map detailing the legendary journey from end to end featured in the Route 66 Plaza. The flat, paved trail offers a nice, fast hike that offers up a bit of state and ecological history along with a variety of features to be enjoyed by all ages.

Distance: 1.5-mile loop
Hiking time: About 1 hour
Difficulty: Easy
Trail surface: Asphalt paved path
Best season: Year-round
Other trail users: Joggers
Canine compatibility: Leashed dogs permitted
Fees and permits: None
Schedule: Dawn to dusk

Maps: Oklahoma City Parks and Recreation Dept., (405) 297-2211; www.okc.gov/parks/route_66/index.html
Trail contact: Oklahoma City Parks and Recreation Dept., 420 W. Main, Oklahoma City, OK 73102, (405) 297-2211; www.okc.gov/parks/route_66/index.html

Finding the trailhead: Route 66 Park is located on the west side of Lake Overholser. Take the N. Council Road exit heading north from I-40. Turn left onto NW 10th Street (west). Turn right onto Country Line Road. Turn left onto Overholser Drive, then left onto NW 23rd Street. You will see the colorful red, yellow and green retro-looking park entrance sign on your right. Turn right onto Andy Payne Lane to enter into park. GPS: N35 29.767' / W97 41.483'

The Hike

Even on a hot summer's day, strolling this park offers up some of the finest images of the heartland. Gaze up toward the powder-blue sky swept with puffy milk-white clouds, then look out along the horizon, where you can see fields of alfalfa waving in a drift of afternoon wind. This image reflects the "sea" of the Great Plains states, where wheat and other types of grain flow for miles and miles anchored within the heartland of America.

The Oklahoma City star medallion is the center point of the detailed Route 66 map in the plaza. The plaza is the beginning of this hike, but you can begin at any point near the plaza and follow the trail that wraps around the park. Make sure to wander around the plaza and read the rest of the markers placed along the map.

Walking along the path, you will have a chance to see and visit many of the park's features, such as the largest playground in the Parks and Recreation system and the three-story observation tower, where you can view the 148-acre park's ponds and nearby Lake Overholser. In addition, there is a skate court, an amphitheater, and a covered picnic pavilion.

Walk near the ponds toward the entrance of the park as you follow the trail, and you will surely see ducks in the water or waddling about; it seems every pond in Oklahoma City is home to a family of ducks. Another interesting feature of the park is the ecological educational signage set along the wetland boardwalks, bridges, and plantings. Kids can learn about the value of the local wetlands within their

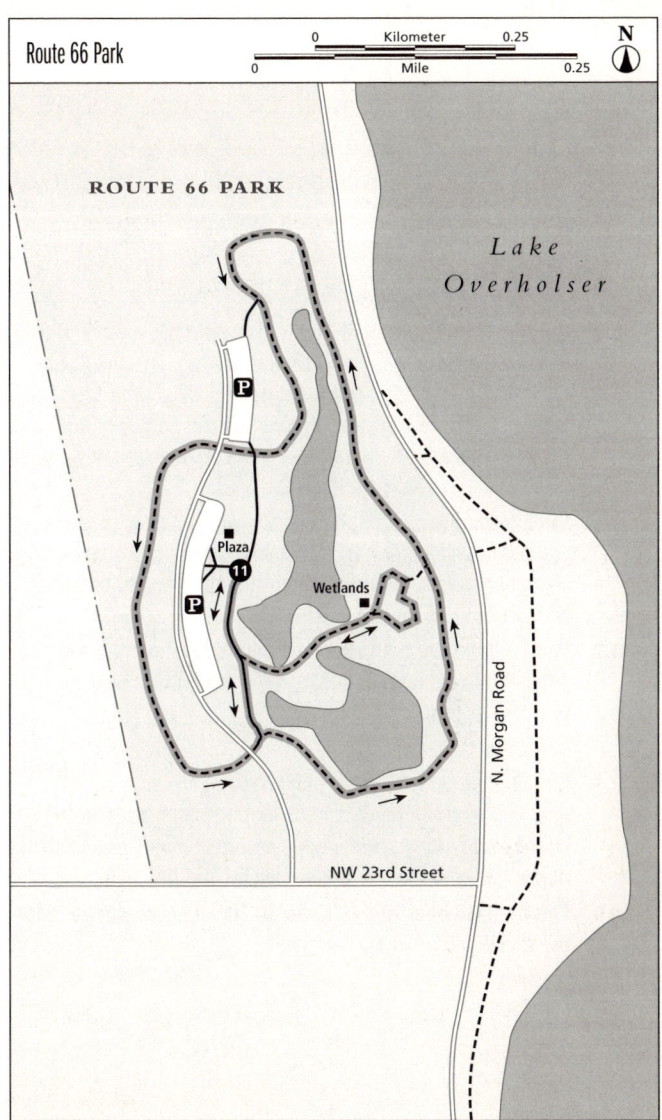

Route 66 Park

ROUTE 66 PARK

Lake Overholser

Plaza

11

Wetlands

N. Morgan Road

NW 23rd Street

0   Kilometer   0.25

0   Mile   0.25

N

environment, for example. Interpretive signs strategically placed around the boardwalk offer information and tips like "How to Take Care of Our Wetlands." Continue walking along the asphalt trail all the way around the park, taking time out to read the interpretive signs along the way. You may want to add to your mileage by taking on a hike of Lake Overholser, which is within sight from the trailhead.

Miles and Directions

0.0 Start from the parking lot and walk toward the middle of the Route 66 Plaza area. Stop at the center point of the Route 66 trail stamped map inlay that depicts Oklahoma City. The inlay is a picture icon story chronicling the origins of Route 66 from Chicago to Santa Monica in Los Angeles. Begin the hike from this history marker.

0.1 Stroll toward the small pond on the wide asphalt trail, where you might encounter migrating birds, ducks, and cranes skimming across the pond. Cross a small wooden bridge as you head to the Wetlands area.

0.2 Wind around the path and veer right to connect with the small Wetlands loop and take in the interpretive signs.

0.4 Walk around the loop. Turn left to connect and continue along the main trail.

0.7 Continue around the main trail bordering the park or you may connect with the Wetlands loop to return back to the starting point for a shorter hike. As you continue this stretch of the trail, you will see a pumping oil-and-gas well.

1.5 End the hike back at the Route 66 Trail Inlay, or continue to the parking lot.

12 Downtown Urban Museum Trail

Since 2000 downtown Oklahoma City has transformed into an urban hub of activity for residents and tourists alike. This hike circles the center of the activity, beginning at the Myriad Botanical Gardens and continuing along the city streets to the Oklahoma City Memorial and art museums. This short trail provides a combination cultural hiking overview of the revitalized city.

Distance: 1.7-mile one-way
Hiking time: About 1.3 hours
Difficulty: Easy and flat
Trail surface: Asphalt and concrete city sidewalks
Best season: Year-round
Other trail users: Pedestrians
Canine compatibility: Leashed dogs permitted

Fees and permits: None
Schedule: Dawn to dusk
Maps: http://myriadgardens.com/maps.html
Trail contacts: www.oklahomacitynationmemorial.org
Other: Bricktown district is a good neighborhood extension add-on.

Finding the trailhead: From the metro Oklahoma City area, drive south on I-235/US 77 toward downtown Oklahoma City. Exit westbound N. 6th Street (exit 1F). Turn right onto NE 6th Street. Take the second left onto N. Broadway Avenue, which becomes E. K. Gaylord Boulevard. Turn right onto W. Sheridan Avenue. Across the street you will see the Cox Convention Center. Look for parking in the area. Begin the hike at the corner of Robinson and Sheridan at the edge of Myriad Botanical Gardens, near the fountain. Start here for better access due to ongoing construction in the area. This route may be altered due to heavy ongoing construction in the downtown area. GPS: N35 27.979' / W97 30.967'

The Hike

With the enhancement of art museums, the Bricktown entertainment district and the Arts District, the Oklahoma City Memorial, and the revival of Myriad Botanical Gardens, spending a long day hiking the urban center offers a full day of sensory input. Begin the hike at the fountain located on the edge of the gardens at the corner of Robinson and Sheridan. Plan to spend extra time strolling around the gardens either before or after the hike. There are 17 acres of carefully tended garden displays to enjoy as well as the crown jewel, the Crystal Bridge Tropical Conservatory. Tropics in the middle of the prairie? Yes, indeed! A jungle environment thrives within the 224-foot-long circular crystal conservatory complete with towering palm trees, exotic plantings, and crashing waterfalls. You will even see species of exotic jungle wildlife such as birds, butterflies, fish, and loads of amphibians and reptiles.

As you follow the route, traipsing the sidewalks down Broadway, there are signs with directional arrows indicating the location of the Oklahoma City National Memorial and Museum. Continue along this trail to reach the memorial. Before you reach the memorial, you will pass a few small fountain gardens. Benches are nearby if you would like to stop and rest. The signs and this trail lead directly into the outdoor symbolic memorial through one of the two formal entrances. Be prepared for a powerful learning experience on the impact of terrorism as you continue. If you have time, visit the museum before walking the outdoor grounds, as it offers the story of the Oklahoma City bombing of the Alfred P. Murrah Federal Building that took place on April 19, 1995. The memorial honors the victims, survivors, rescuers, and all the community that was changed forever on that day. Especially poignant is the field of 168 empty chairs, one for each life lost, overlooking the reflecting pool.

After leaving the memorial, head back on the trail, continuing until you reach the Arts District, which is just a few blocks from the memorial. You will pass by the Oklahoma City Museum of Art toward your left. If you are not too overwhelmed from sensory overload at this point, check out the museum's stunning collection of Chihuly glass. From the street you can see through the modern building's massive window the two-story Chihuly Waterford Crystal Chandelier.

The trail heads back to the Myriad Gardens, where you can end your hike with an afternoon Shakespeare Festival performance at the amphitheater or conclude with an evening Concert in the Park during their summer series.

Miles and Directions

0.0 Begin at the corner of Robinson and Sheridan at the edge of Myriad Gardens. From the fountain walk east on the sidewalk.

0.12 Turn left at the light onto Broadway Avenue and follow the sidewalk. Follow sidewalk signs leading to Oklahoma City Memorial. Continue on Broadway Avenue.

0.6 Turn left at 5th Street. A sidewalk sign points you in the direction of the OKC Memorial.

0.7 At this point you will be standing in front of one of the two entrance gates into the outdoor OKC Memorial. Walk past the entrance and continue into the memorial. It is free to enter the outdoor memorial grounds.

0.8 As you walk across the grounds, you will notice the reflecting pool. The design of the chairs facing the pool were constructed as a memorial to each of the victims that died

Downtown Urban Museum Trail

| 0 | | Kilometer | | 0.25 |
| 0 | | Mile | | 0.25 |

N

NW 7th St.

N. Walker Ave.

N. Hudson Ave.

N. Harvey Ave.

NW 6th St.

OKC National Memorial

NW 5th St.

NW 4th St.

NW 4th St.

Dean A. McGee Ave.

Courthouse

N. Robinson Ave.

N. Broadway Ave.

NW 2nd St.

Arts District

OKC Museum of Art

Park Ave.

N.E.K. Gaylord Blvd.

W. Main St.

Dewey Ave.

N. Walker Ave.

W. Sheridan Ave.

To Bricktown

12

Crystal Bridge Tropical Conservatory

S. Robinson Ave.

Cox Convention Center

Myriad Botanical Gardens

W. Reno Ave.

SW 2nd St.

240

S. Harvey Ave.

SW 3rd St.

240

SW 4th St.

as a result of the bombing of the Alfred P. Murrah Federal Building. Keep walking to the other side of the grounds and exit the gate. Turn left after exiting the memorial. Follow the sidewalk and continue walking.

1.2 Cross the street and turn left on Walker Avenue, continuing on Walker. This area is known as the Arts District. You will see the OKC Museum of Art as you continue walking.

1.3 From the street you will see how the modern design of the building blends with the older architecture of the buildings nearby. Notice the striking, full two-story window display showcasing the Chihuly glass artwork.

1.6 Turn left in front of the very contemporary building, which is a local theater (half a block before Reno). Step onto the brick walkway that opens into a small city performing arts plaza. Follow the brick walkway to the Crystal Bridge of Myriad Gardens, which you will see directly in front of you.

1.7 Cross the street to arrive at Myriad Gardens and the end of the hike.

Option: If you still have energy, add some more mileage to your hike by walking the paths around the gardens.

13 Oklahoma River Trail: North

This tree-lined, smooth-as-silk asphalt trail offers up splendid skyline views of Oklahoma City, beginning from downtown Regatta Park and then following the tame Oklahoma River. At the end of the one-way route, hikers can either double-back along the North Trail or venture back along the South Trail to the starting point, which adds another 7.0 miles to the hike.

Distance: 5.7 miles one-way
Hiking time: About 2.5 hours
Difficulty: Easy and flat
Trail surface: Asphalt
Best season: Year-round
Other trail users: Cyclists, in-line skaters, skateboarders, joggers
Canine compatibility: Leashed dogs permitted
Fees and permits: None
Schedule: Dawn to dusk

Maps: Detailed map available for download from www.okc.gov/trails/n_canadian.html or www.okc.gov/trails/river_trails_map.pdf
Special considerations: Direct overhead sun at midday with no cover
Trail contact: Oklahoma City Parks and Recreations Department, 420 W. Main, Oklahoma City, OK 73102, (405) 297-2211

Finding the trailhead: Take I-35 south to I-40 east. Exit Reno Avenue (east) and drive for 1.5 miles. Turn left on S. Lincoln Boulevard and continue for 0.4 mile. The trail begins from N. Regatta Park, which is off Byers Avenue, just west of the Byers Avenue Bridge. The street address is 725 S. Lincoln Blvd. The parking lot can be accessed from either I-40 or I-35 by taking the Lincoln Boulevard exit (south). GPS: N35 27.501' / W97 30.234'

The Hike

The Boathouse District is one of the most diverse outdoor multisport excursion centers in Oklahoma City and is an excellent destination for an extended weekend visit. It is within walking distance of the Bricktown District and the Downtown Urban Museum Trail (Hike 12). And the Boathouse District is also the future site for an Adventure Zip Line over the river and construction is now in the works for the OKC Riversport Sky Trail and Youth Pavilion.

The Devon Boathouse perched along the banks of the Oklahoma River provides the starting point for the pleasant hike along the North Trail and adds a special element to the outdoor experience. Visitors can take a tour of the boathouse and learn about kayaking or rowing. This hike begins with a walk-through of the Devon Boathouse, which gives visitors the opportunity to learn more if they wish about this growing sport in OKC. You might be wondering, "Rowing in Oklahoma?" Not only is it true, but the US Olympic Committee has recognized the Oklahoma River as a US Olympic and Paralympic Training Site. So along the hiking trail you will see views of waterway attractions, parks, and wetland areas, and if luck prevails, you might spot Olympic hopefuls rowing in preparation for a race.

As you walk along the route, you will notice that there are no motorized vehicle crossings, which also makes it a comfortable trail for those with disabilities who use mobility aids. As you walk you will pass a railway overpass and might glimpse chugging trains along the tracks. The route also passes by the historic Oklahoma National Stockyards, which was founded in 1910 and is considered a favorite destination for tourists seeking an authentic cow-town experience. You

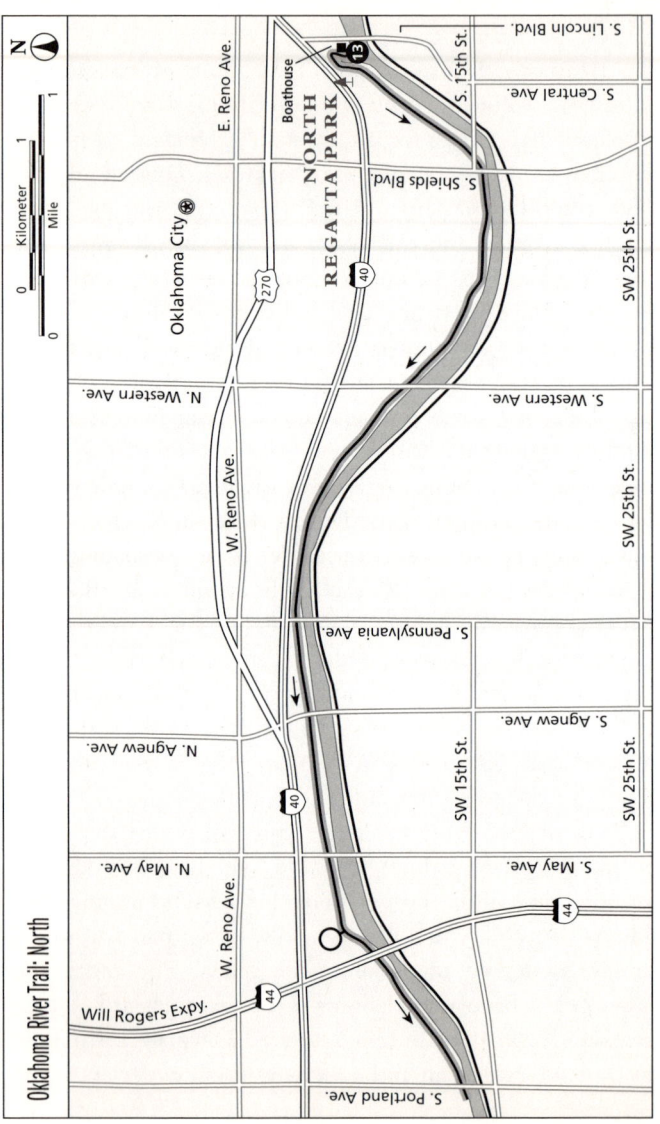

Oklahoma River Trail: North

N

Will Rogers Expy.

W. Reno Ave.

N. May Ave.

N. Agnew Ave.

N. Western Ave.

W. Reno Ave.

Oklahoma City

E. Reno Ave.

Boathouse

NORTH REGATTA PARK

S. Shields Blvd.

S. Portland Ave.

S. May Ave.

S. Agnew Ave.

SW 15th St.

SW 25th St.

S. Pennsylvania Ave.

S. Western Ave.

SW 25th St.

SW 25th St.

S. Central Ave.

S. 15th St.

S. Lincoln Blvd

13

Kilometer

Mile

0   1

0   1

can find behemoth-size beef steaks at Cattlemen's Cafe and the best western boot selection at Langston's Westernwear.

At any point you could turn around and go back to the trailhead, but if you wish to continue and finish the trail, be cautioned that it does dead-end.

Miles and Directions

0.0 Begin from the Regatta boat station center. Follow steps to the left to view the boat station.

0.2 Enter the building to view the boathouse.

0.5 Continue on the wide, multiuse path facing the river. Follow the path to your right.

1.2 Look at overpass above you to see the railway for passing trains.

1.5 Arrive at one of the crossover points to access the South Oklahoma River Trail. Continue along the path or cross over at this point to connect with the South Trail. The trail hugs the river.

3.3 Look for athletes training on the river. You may see a rowing team practicing for the Olympics. This is also a good place to see a glimpse of Stockyards City in the distance as you continue walking.

5.3 Arrive at the last access point from the North Trail to the South Trail connection.

5.7 The trail ends at the roundabout. You may want to park another car in the area if you prefer not to double-back to the beginning and/or possibly connect with the South Trail for a longer hike.

14 Red Rock Canyon State Park: California Nature Trail (Plus Extension)

In the 1800s this sandstone canyon oasis was used by settlers heading west to California in their covered wagons as a stopping waypoint. The California Nature Trail is located on the west side of the canyon and still bears wagon-wheel ruts imprinted in the red rocks. This hike is demanding due to a brief incline and descent on rugged rock formations.

Distance: 2.4-mile circuit
Hiking time: About 2.5 hours
Difficulty: Moderate
Trail surface: Rugged rock and dirt, forested trail
Best season: Spring through fall
Other trail users: None
Canine compatibility: Leashed dogs permitted but not advised due to terrain
Fees and permits: None
Schedule: Park open 24 hours daily

Maps: www.travelok.com/listings/view.profile/id.6275
Trail contact: Visitor Center, Highway 281 South, Hinton, OK 73047, (405) 542-6344
Other: Pool open during summer season from Memorial Day to Labor Day. Fee required to swim. Campsites and RV campground are available to reserve for a fee. Five picnic shelters are located throughout the park.
E-mail: redrockcanyon@oklahomaparks.com

Finding the trailhead: The state park is set in the canyon surrounded by red rock walls. About a 1-hour drive from Oklahoma City. Take I-40 West toward Hinton and exit 101 (US 281/OK 8 exit), then turn south and continue 5.2 miles on Highway 28. Turn left into the entrance of the park. The hike starts at the west end of the canyon. From the main park road, drive past the pool on your right. Continue past the rappelling rock face area toward the parking area next to the CALIFORNIA WAGON TRAIL sign. GPS: N35 26.357' / W98 21.300'

The Hike

Driving across the plains toward Hinton in west-central Oklahoma, you would never guess that there is a stunning red rock canyon within its midst. The state park is set in the canyon, surrounded by red rock walls. After entering the state park the road quickly and steeply descends into a canyon oasis that would tickle the fancy of any outdoor enthusiast.

Walk about 75 yards behind the sign along the meadow toward the canyon wall. You will notice the beginning of the rugged rock and rusty-red hard-packed dirt trail leading upward. There is a short but steep ascent up the trail to an overlook. Handrails are provided for much of the way for balance and support if needed. Follow the rock trail until you come to an embedded branded cement circle in the rock with CRT carved into the circle. The initials stand for California Road Trail with an arrow pointing right. Follow the direction of the arrow. On this route it is very important to observe the trail markers indicating CRT and follow the arrows as there are no marked trails other than the California Nature Trail. This hike extends from the CRT following the forested dirt path, where oak and red cedar trees embrace the trail on either side, providing much needed shade during hot summer days. The trail narrows and widens as it winds around the top of the canyon walls.

There are many spurs off of the main trail that you can take at your own discretion. Some spurs lead directly down the canyon walls to the park below, allowing you to cut your hike short. This hike continues around toward the other side of the park near the entrance. Of all the hikes in this guide, this is the most challenging as the trail offers a variety of terrain, including climbing briefly up and down rock surfaces.

For an amazing fall foliage show, hike the trail from mid-October through the first part of November. You will be treated to a blaze of color that includes the rare Caddo maple tree, which is native to the area. Vibrant shades of red, orange, and yellow leaves provide a gorgeous canopy for hiking among the red rocks.

Eventually the trail leads to the very top of the smooth sandstone surface and you will be able to take in views across the canyon to the other side and of the park below. There are a number of access points to hike down the red rock walls. Be careful along the edge—it is not recommended to walk along the edge of the canyon walls. Follow the curve of the red rock around; it is shaped like a horseshoe. You will see a spur that leads down onto the main camp road. The short descent down is rugged and rocky, making this one of the most difficult sections of the trail.

Miles and Directions

0.0 The trailhead is in back of the CALIFORNIA WAGON TRAIL sign (at about 75 yards). There is a very short red rock trail you must climb. There are handrails if you need support. Follow the rock trail.

0.05 Embedded in the rock, you will see a branded cement circle with the initials CRT (California Road Trail) carved into the circle. There is an arrow pointing right. Follow the direction of the arrow.

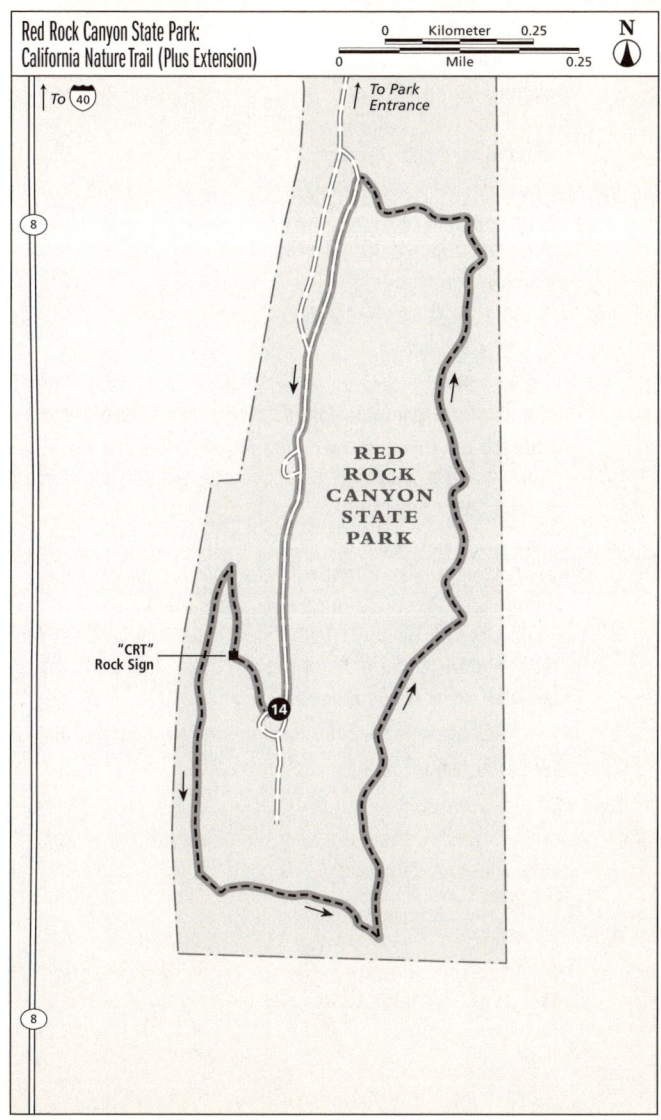

Red Rock Canyon State Park:
California Nature Trail (Plus Extension)

0   Kilometer   0.25

0   Mile   0.25

N

↑ To 40

↑ To Park
Entrance

8

RED
ROCK
CANYON
STATE
PARK

"CRT"
Rock Sign

14

8

0.4 The trail switches back and forth and changes from rocky paths to hard-packed dirt trails throughout the remainder of the hike. At this point you will notice the fenced-off park boundary on the right and the thick forest growth on the other side of the trail. Be watchful for snakes along the trail, including rattlesnakes.

0.7 You will descend again along red rock and come into another shaded forested area with thick tree growth. Follow the trail as it cuts across through a meadow and continues on cross-country terrain.

1.1 The trail continues along red rocks and open meadow.

1.8 You will discover large red rock outcroppings and tremendous views of the canyon below. Walk carefully along the red rock and continue toward your right, connecting with the sandy red dirt trail mixed with red rocks. At this point you will be hiking at the top of the red rock walls and can see the park below you.

2.1 Follow the curve of the red rock as it connects with the dirt trail, leading to a spur that continues down onto the main camp road. There are a number of spurs that lead down into the park below. Be very careful on your descent as it can be steep with rocks and roots of trees to negotiate as you pick your path down to the ground.

2.4 Walk back along the Main Camp Road to your car and the end of the hike.

15 Roman Nose State Park: Inspiration Point Trail

Reach the top of the point and you will discover the meaning behind the name of the trail. Inspiring indeed! The lookout is one of the highest points in the area, with a panoramic view that spans for miles. The valley below is a good place to observe how gypsum rock plays a part in shaping these canyons.

Distance: 3.5-mile circuit
Hiking time: About 2 hours
Difficulty: Easy to moderate
Trail surface: Hard-packed dirt
Best season: Apr through Nov
Other trail users: Equestrians and mountain bikers
Canine compatibility: Leashed dogs permitted
Fees and permits: None
Schedule: Dawn to dusk year-round
Maps: www.travelok.com/listings/view.profile/id.6460
Trail contacts: Roman Nose State Park, (580) 623-4218 or (800) 892-8690, fax (580) 623-2190; lodge office, (800) 892-8690; General Store, (580) 623-7750
Other: Recreational activities include swimming pools, 2 lakes, trout fishing in season, canoeing, paddleboats, mountain biking, horse stables, and hayrides by reservation. Rentals include canoes, kayaks, paddleboats, and mountain bikes. Group camps, picnic areas, tent campsites, and RV campsites with hookups and teepee rentals are located throughout the park. The 22-room Roman Nose Lodge has been renovated to incorporate the area's natural surroundings and offers a restaurant and great views from the lobby lounge deck.

Finding the trailhead: The park is located on OK 8A, 7.0 miles north of the town of Watonga. From Oklahoma City drive I-40 west.

Exit on US 281 Spur North, exit 108, toward Geary/Watonga. Turn right onto US 281 Spur/South, Walbaum Road. Continue to follow US 281 Spur West as it becomes OK 8 North. Continue until you reach the park entrance. Follow signs to Roman Nose Lodge. Park in the lodge parking lot. The trailhead is a few feet from the parking lot beginning at the OH LET ME ROAM trail sign. GPS: N35 56.156' / W98 25.472'

The Hike

Named after the Southern Cheyenne chief Henry Roman Nose, Roman Nose State Park offers captivating scenery with trails covering a vast geological landscape of rocky cliffs; gypsum, shale, and dolomite ledges; steep-walled canyons; grassy mesas topped with trees; creeks; ravines; lakes; and freshwater natural springs. If you only have time for one hike in the park, this is the one to explore. You will discover all the elements described above while enjoying the trail except for the natural springs, which is best observed by taking the Three Springs Trail (Hike 17).

Many of the trails can be accessed from the Roman Nose State Park Lodge parking lot, including this one. Start at the OH LET ME ROAM sign posted next to the parking lot, where the trail leads onto a woodsy, tree-covered path and crosses creeks over a few wooden bridges. Use caution after a rain as the wooden slats might be slick. But take in the aroma of the spicy damp earth and the scent of cedar. Oklahoma is blessed, or cursed as some locals would admit, with an overabundance of red cedar trees proliferating across the plains. Although these fast-growing trees shelter the trail, their original purpose was as a "windbreak" planted next to homes by settlers after staking their claim during the land rush days in the late nineteenth century. Nowadays the red cedar tree is considered a weed and a bit of a nuisance, creating havoc with the indigenous natural habitat of the plains.

Continue on the path and you might be serenaded by cicadas and birdsong along the way. And if you are lucky, perhaps an array of dragonflies will flutter nearby, displaying the colorful paint jobs on their wings. You will come to the PROSPEROUS POPULATIONS trail marker, which offers information on the area and gives the option to go left onto the Two Lakes hike. This is a nice short hike to do at sunset for lovely mesa views. Turn right to continue on the Inspiration Point hike.

The trail winds along grassy mesas and up and down hard-packed red dirt and along gypsum white rock single-track paths. Continue upward along a plateau until you reach the top of the point. The "lookout" provides an amazing view of the valley below and the plains beyond. This very pretty picture-postcard point offers views of buttes to one side, with Lake Watonga on the other side, and colorful red shale and white gypsum rock forming the canyon walls stretching out across the perimeter. The horizontal rock striations are really interesting, forming a layer cake of color.

Follow the trail down along the hard-packed dirt toward the Rock Garden of red rock boulders, and continue along the lake, where the trail becomes very narrow, hugs the lakeshore, then leads you back to the main trail. Double-back along the main trail, ending at the parking lot of the lodge.

Miles and Directions

0.0   Begin at the OH LET ME ROAM trail marker from the lodge parking lot.

0.07 After crossing a wooden bridge along the forested path, you will reach the PROSPEROUS POPULATIONS trail marker. Turn right

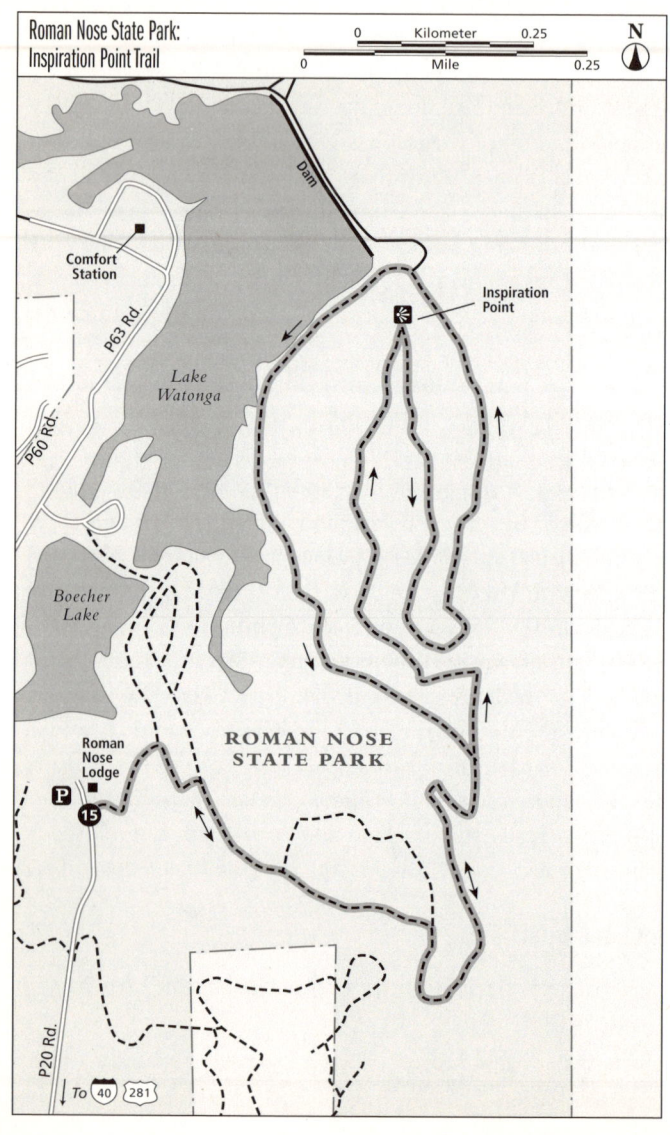

Roman Nose State Park:
Inspiration Point Trail

0   Kilometer   0.25

0   Mile   0.25

N

Comfort
Station

P63 Rd.

P60 Rd.

Dam

Lake
Watonga

Inspiration
Point

Boecher
Lake

Roman
Nose
Lodge

P

15

ROMAN NOSE
STATE PARK

P20 Rd.

To 40 281

at the sign and continue on the dirt and white gypsum rock path.

0.3 Continue along the main trail. If you would like to add a quarter-mile extension to your hike, take the Canyon Spur to your left. It will loop back to the main trail.

0.4 This section offers a very short but steep climb up packed red dirt. If it's wet, it could be slippery in spots.

0.5 Veer right on the trail. You will observe a variety of trees, such as red cedar, mixed in with cacti along the sides of the trail.

0.6 Veer left to continue on the Inspiration Trail.

1.0 Veer right on the trail and hike upward toward Inspiration Point.

1.5 You are at the lookout viewing area for Inspiration Point. Observe the beautiful panoramic view of the whole valley from your perch on the point. Notice how the gypsum rock plays a part in shaping the canyons. Then continue on the trail leading down through red rocks and eventually meeting up with the lake.

2.4 Continue along the trail, hugging the lake.

2.9 The winding lake trail eventually connects back to the main trail. Double-back along the main trail to the starting point.

3.5 End the hike back at the lodge parking lot.

16 Roman Nose State Park: Lake Dam Trail

One of the most popular state parks in Oklahoma since its inception in 1937, Roman Nose State Park has been an entertaining outdoor wonderland for generations of families in the area. This easy, flat, grassy trail is perfect for families with small children. Wildlife tracks can be seen along the trail and near the dam, offering an overview of the types of animals that can be found in the park.

Distance: 1.6 miles out and back

Hiking time: About 1 hour

Difficulty: Easy

Trail surface: Hard-packed dirt

Best season: Apr through Nov

Other trail users: Mountain bikers

Canine compatibility: Leashed dogs permitted

Fees and permits: None

Schedule: Dawn to dusk year-round

Maps: www.travelok.com/listings/view.profile/id.6460

Trail contacts: Roman Nose State Park, (580) 623-4218 or (800) 892-8690, fax (580) 623-2190; lodge office, (800) 892-8690; General Store, (580) 623-7750

Other: Recreational activities include swimming pools, 2 lakes, trout fishing in season, canoeing, paddleboats, mountain biking, horse stables, and hayrides by reservation. Rentals include canoes, kayaks, paddleboats, and mountain bikes. Group camps, picnic areas, tent campsites, and RV campsites with hookups and teepee rentals are located throughout the park. The 22-room Roman Nose Lodge has been renovated to incorporate the area's natural surroundings and offers a restaurant and great views from the lobby lounge deck.

Finding the trailhead: The park is located on OK 8A, 7.0 miles north of the town of Watonga. From Oklahoma City drive I-40 west. Exit on US 281 Spur North, exit 108, toward Geary/Watonga. Turn right onto US 281 Spur/South, Walbaum Road. Continue to follow US 281 Spur West as it becomes OK 8 North. Continue until you reach the park entrance. Follow the signs to the General Store and the Lake Loop Trail. Park near the Lake Loop Trail area lots. GPS: N35 56.593' / W98 25.529'

The Hike

Long before it was a state park, this canyon landscape was the campsite of Southern Cheyenne Chief Henry Roman Nose. Indian lodges were protected by canyon walls from the cold winter winds. Freshwater was plentiful, with the springs and lakes nearby, and bison still roamed the grassy plains. Today visitors to the park can view a sign placed in honor of the chief that describes the location of the original campground. The parking lot for the Lake Loop trailhead marker is near the sign.

Instead of taking the Lake Loop, this hike covers a short trail to the end of the dam and doubles back to the start. The hike is a particularly good one for hikers who require a more flat, even surface as it is mostly a grassy, dirt-packed trail. The wide, flat, packed-dirt trail is as wide as a fire trail (about 6 feet) and provides a great canvas for animal track imprints. Look for raccoon, bobcat, deer, or coyote tracks.

Follow the trail from the Lake Loop trail marker and continue along the path until you reach a tall grassy meadow toward your left. This area is also great for spotting wild-life tracks. Before you set out be sure to pick up a printed document from the information center created by the park rangers that displays wildlife tracks and how to identify the

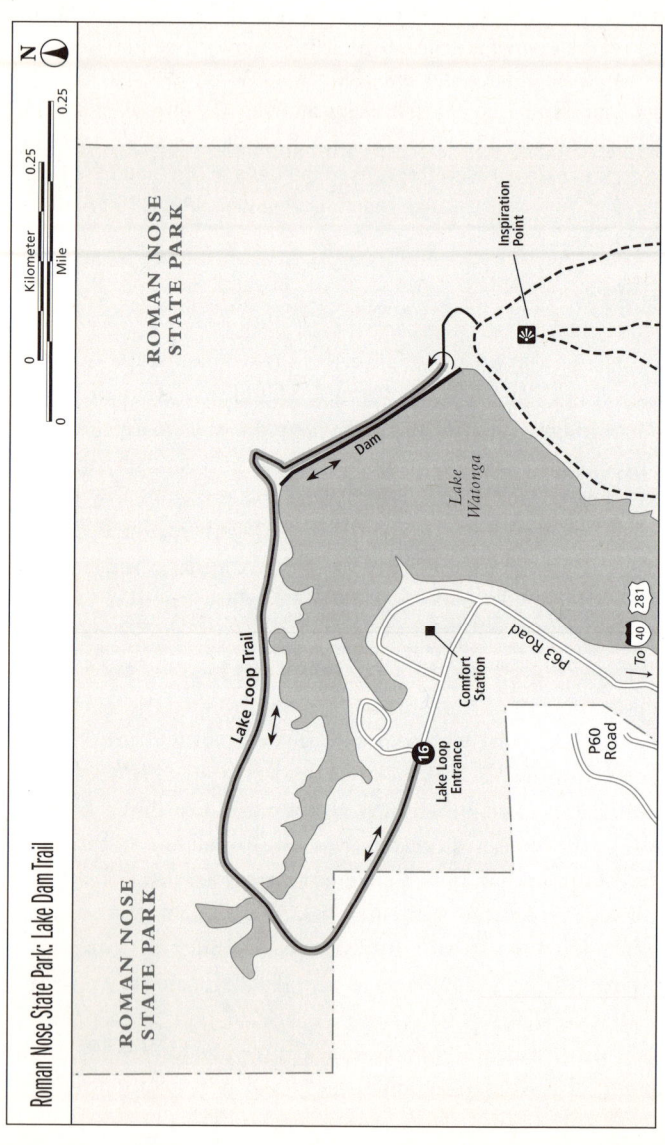

Roman Nose State Park: Lake Dam Trail

ROMAN NOSE STATE PARK

ROMAN NOSE STATE PARK

Lake Loop Trail

Dam

Lake Watonga

Inspiration Point

16 Lake Loop Entrance

Comfort Station

P63 Road

To 40 281

P60 Road

N

0   0.25   Kilometer
0   0.25   Mile

animals associated with the tracks. The brochure is a great learning tool to take along on a hike with children.

After exploring the meadow return to the grassy path over the dam. Continue toward the end of the main path. Lake Watonga is in view on your right, and to the other side is Bitter Creek. At the end of the dam, turn around and walk back to the trailhead.

Miles and Directions

0.0 Start the hike at the Lake Loop Trail marker. Follow the wide, flat, packed-dirt trail.

0.7 Veer left from the dam trail onto a small grassy meadow. Directly in front of the meadow is a canyon overlook. Depending on the season, you might see cattails pointing upward toward the sky among the tallgrass. Look for animal tracks along the stream beds as you make your way back to the main trail.

0.8 A short walk brings you to the end of the dam trail. Turn around and walk back to the beginning of the trailhead.

1.6 End the hike back at the trailhead.

17 Roman Nose State Park: Three Springs Trail

This is by far the shortest hike in the book but definitely one of the richest in terms of beauty. The Three Springs Trail is not to be missed. Each spring is situated within an enchanting riparian environment literally within steps of one another.

Distance: 0.3-mile circuit
Hiking time: About 30 minutes
Difficulty: Easy
Trail surface: Dirt and forest trail
Best season: Year-round
Other trail users: None
Canine compatibility: Leashed dogs permitted
Fees and permits: None
Schedule: Dawn to dusk year-round
Maps: www.travelok.com/listings/view.profile/id.6460
Trail contacts: Roman Nose State Park, (580) 623-4218 or (800) 892-8690, fax (580) 623-2190; lodge office, (800) 892-8690; General Store, (580) 623-7750

Other: Recreational activities include swimming pools, 2 lakes, trout fishing in season, canoeing, paddleboats, mountain biking, horse stables, and hayrides by reservation. Rentals include canoes, kayaks, paddleboats, and mountain bikes. Group camps, picnic areas, tent camp-sites, and RV campsites with hookups and teepee rentals are located throughout the park. The 22-room Roman Nose Lodge has been renovated to incorporate the area's natural surroundings and offers a restaurant and great views from the lobby lounge deck.

Finding the trailhead: The park is located on OK 8A, 7.0 miles north of the town of Watonga. From Oklahoma City drive I-40 west.

Exit on US 281 Spur North, exit 108, toward Geary/Watonga. Turn right onto US 281 Spur/South, Walbaum Road. Continue to follow US 281 Spur West. as it becomes OK 8 North. Continue until you reach the park entrance. Follow the park road until you reach a fork with signs for the Bittercreek Canyon recreational area: Pool, Picnic and Springs Area. Turn left and follow the signs to the pool parking lot. GPS: N35 55.962' / W98 26.418'

The Hike

It's not hard to imagine that this was a popular stop for settlers traveling west or as a campsite location for Indians over a century ago. The springs provided a continuous supply of freshwater and continue to be a restorative stopping place for visitors.

The area is known as Bittercreek Canyon. Big Spring, Middle Spring, and Little Spring are connected by a pathway that can be accessed at different points. This hike begins from the parking lot nearest the swimming pool. Walk down the stone steps to the small park area, where you will see picnic tables dotting the grassy lawn to your left and the rock bathhouse to your right along with the swimming pool. You will be tempted to visit the pool after the hike. Both the rock bathhouse and the pool were constructed in 1938. Blending in with the environment, the large circular pool is framed by natural rocks nestled against a canyon wall. Most of the structures in the Three Springs area are original and hand-built with native stone.

Follow the wide, paved path or take the grassy trail next to the creek that leads up to Big Spring. Walk over the wooden bridge that crosses the creek and continue along the path, where you will glimpse a gentle waterfall from the trail that takes you directly to a stream and small falls. White gypsum rock lines the floor of the creek mingled with tree roots. The canopy of leafy trees shades the springs, allowing for a great rest stop to enjoy the beauty of this little gem. On a hot summer's day, Big Springs is the best place to cool off as the water is reputed to remain at a constant fifty-four degrees Fahrenheit. You will notice near the mouth of a cave a small waterfall that ushers from the natural springs. Along the entrance to the mouth of the cave, you can see colorful striations of white gypsum and red rock shale forming the wall with an overlay of clinging tree roots.

After sitting for a while in the shade and cool of the stream, head back to the trail, which is a single-track forested dirt path, and continue on to Middle Springs, the "Crawdad Hole" as it is locally known. Years ago local kids played near the pond and caught crawdads there. The pond looks like it was created from a storybook, with trickling water lapping over stones and dragonflies flitting about. This is a charming natural area to visit and pretend you are Tom Sawyer for a day. Little Springs is nearby, at the end of the trail.

You will see natural stone and rock steps leading up to a beautifully constructed natural rock picnic pavilion and shelter, which was the first official building constructed in the park, in 1939. Continue walking up the steps toward the parking lot and walk back to your car.

Miles and Directions

0.0   Begin the hike from the parking lot at the stone stairway that leads down to the picnic area and pool.

0.2   Cross the wooden bridge near the picnic area and continue walking right toward the stream. Cool off, dip your feet in the water, and relax to the sound of the small waterfall. Discover

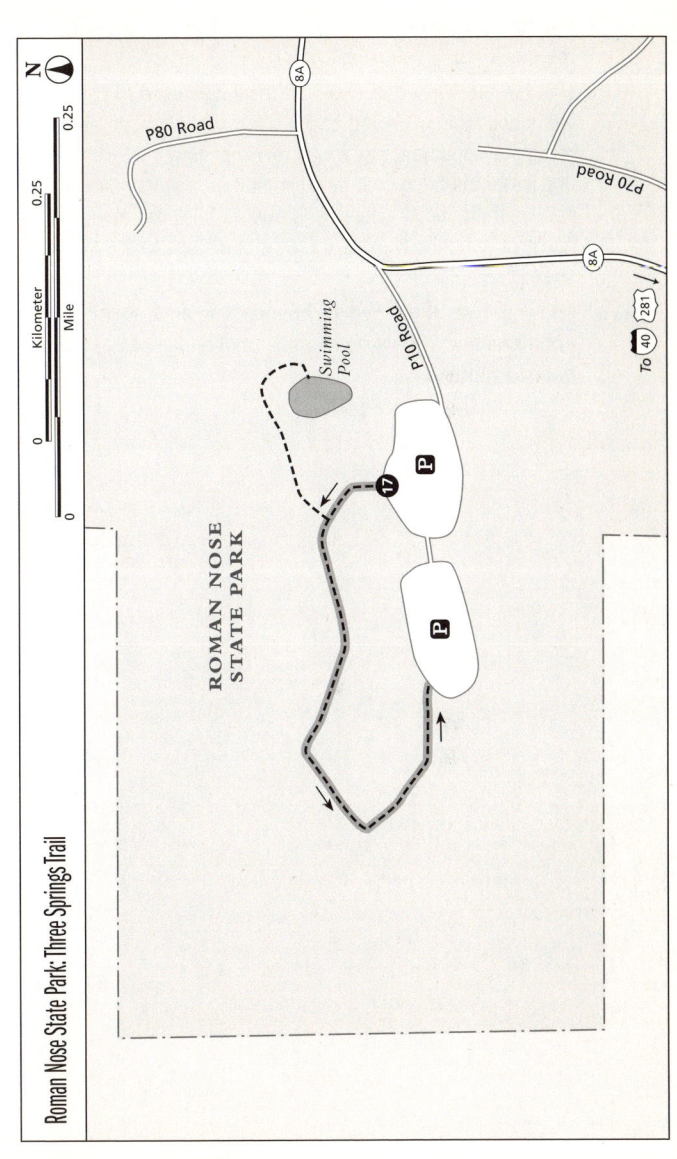

Roman Nose State Park: Three Springs Trail

ROMAN NOSE
STATE PARK

Swimming
Pool

P80 Road

P70 Road

P10 Road

8A

8A

To 40 281

N

Kilometer
0   0.25
Mile
0   0.25

the cave and notice the white gypsum rock on the floor of the creek.

0.26 Head to the "Crawdad Hole," as local kids used to call it years ago. This sheltered spring offers lots of shade and gives the appearance of a natural swimming pool with trickling water tumbling over tiny river stones. At this point you can walk around the creek and double-back the way you came or continue walking up the stone steps to the picnic shelter.

0.3 End your hike at the Service Area parking area, which is approximately 200 yards from the pool parking area. Walk back to your car.

18 Wichita Mountains Wildlife Refuge: Elk Mountain Trail

A gradual uphill trek that winds along forested trail, rocks, and boulder pathways toward one of the highest points on the refuge. Perch on one of the many large boulder outcroppings at the top for a beautiful vista of the refuge, French Lake, and beyond to the plains.

Distance: 2.1 miles out and back

Hiking time: About 2 hours

Difficulty: Easy to moderate due to uphill ascent

Trail surface: Hard-packed dirt and rock path

Best season: Year-round

Other trail users: None

Canine compatibility: Leashed dogs permitted

Fees and permits: None

Schedule: Dawn to dusk

Maps: Go to the U.S. Fish and Wildlife Service website: www.fws.gov/southwest/refuges/oklahoma/wichitamountains/brochuresmaps.html

Trail contacts: Wichita Mountains Wildlife Refuge, 32 Refuge Headquarters, Indiahoma, OK 73552, (580) 429-3222, fax (580) 429-9323. Refuge visitor center is located at the junction of OK 115 and 49.

Special considerations: Be careful as wildlife can be dangerous. Rattlesnakes and copperheads are found in the area. Bison, longhorn cattle, elk, deer, and prairie dogs should be viewed from a safe distance. Do not approach or feed the wildlife. In late summer 2011 a wildfire swept through a portion of the refuge. Much of the grasslands were scorched but started to bounce back immediately with new growth. Wildlife was largely unharmed. WMWR is an enormous swath of land where there is much to discover and explore beyond the burned areas.

Other: With 15 miles of designated hiking trails, there are plenty of hiking options for the day hiker or weekend visitor. Check with the visitor center to see if there are special guided hikes or tours during the time of your visit.

Finding the trailhead: From Oklahoma City drive I-44 south to the Medicine Park/OK 49 exit. Continue on OK 49, going west 10 miles to the refuge gate. Drive OK 49 through the refuge, following signs to Charon's Garden Wilderness Area/Elk Mountain Trail System. Park in Elk Mountain lot. GPS: N34 43.900' / W98 43.421'

The Hike

Part of the adventure of exploring the Wichita Mountains Wildlife Refuge (WMWR) is the drive into the expansive 59,020-acre refuge. There's not a lot of places in the world where you can drive along a two-lane road with a herd of bison munching their way across the prairie on one side of the road and a herd of longhorn cattle on the other. The WMWR is definitely one of the most unique habitats in the United States and is a crown jewel within the state of Oklahoma. You might even be surprised that there are several mountains within the refuge. Mount Pinchot in the Special Use Area is the tallest peak in the park at 2,476 feet, and Mount Scott is the second-tallest mountain in the refuge at 2,464 feet.

The Elk Mountain Trail System offers two trails for hikers: Charon's Garden Trail and Elk Mountain Trail. For the best valley views in the heart of the refuge, head up Elk Mountain Trail, where you will reach the top near 2,225 feet elevation. Don't worry: It's only about 600 feet of ascent for hikers, as you start at about 1,650 feet. This is a well-maintained trail that should be taken at a comfortable pace,

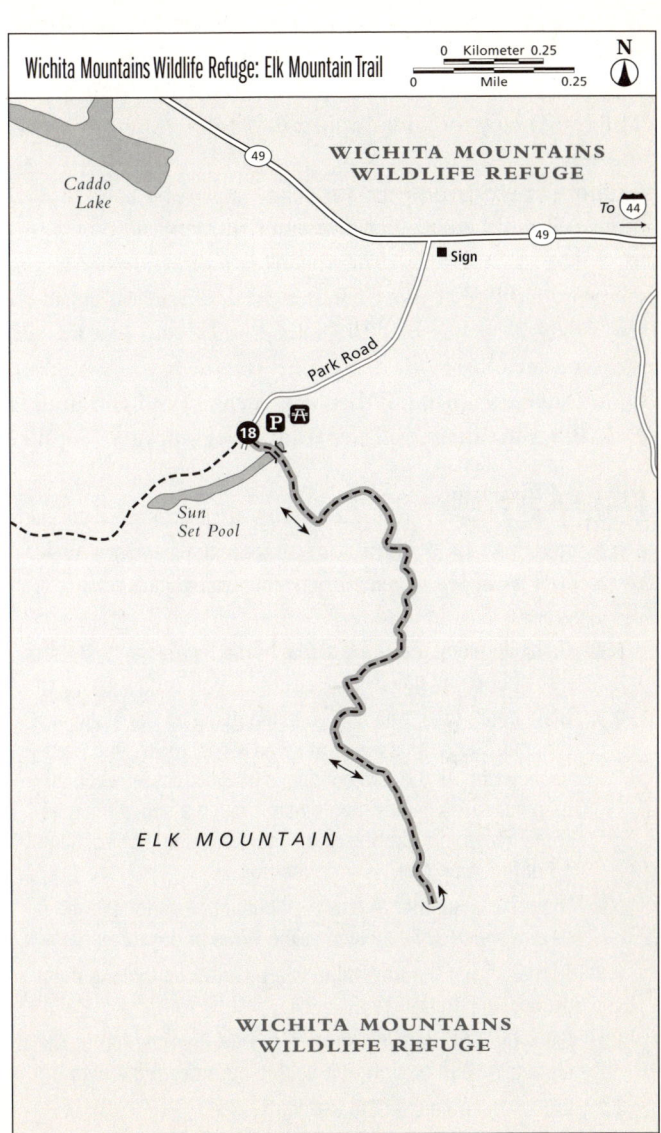

as the route leads uphill for a traverse across boulders, rocks, hard-packed dirt, and forested paths. Keep a close watch on very small children and take your time hiking up to the top. There are many lookout opportunities along the way to stop and rest.

Since there is little to no shade cover, be sure to wear sunscreen and bring plenty of water to drink. The best time to attempt this hike is morning or late afternoon. You may see more wildlife at those times as well. Once you get to the top, you will notice that the trail doesn't end. Toward your right is a meadow with more spurs to take if you would like to continue exploring. Otherwise, turn around and double-back along the main trail toward the beginning of the hike.

Miles and Directions

0.0   Start the hike at the CHARON'S GARDEN trail marker sign. Walk over the bridge onto rock- and stone-cut stairs leading upward.

0.1   Continue along the stone steps, hiking through a shady section of towering oak trees.

0.3   Stay on the main trail and continue going up the stone and dirt trail. The path is a mix of stone steps, rocks, and hard-packed dirt. As the trail continues it levels out in sections, then increases in elevation again through a series of stone steps integrated with the path. There are a number of spurs off of the main trail. Stay on the trail.

0.6   There are a number of nice rock outcroppings to rest and have a snack while looking at the views of the valley below.

0.8   To the right of the trail, there is a picturesque lookout point overlooking the refuge.

1.1   Enjoy the 360-degree panoramic views from the top of Elk Mountain. Turn around and double-back down the path.

2.2   End the hike back at the trailhead.

19 Wichita Mountains Wildlife Refuge: Longhorn Trail

The Longhorn Trail is an easy, flat, grassy, and dirt-packed trail that gives you an idea of how the prairie looked more than a century ago. As you meander along the path, be on the lookout for grazing Texas longhorn cattle or American bison. Remember not to approach the animals. They are more interested in grazing than they are you, but keep a good distance from them. Also, be careful where you step as there could be cow patties (droppings) near the trail.

Distance: 1.5-mile loop
Hiking time: About 1 hour
Difficulty: Easy
Trail surface: Grassy and dirt trail
Best season: Year-round
Other trail users: Hikers
Canine compatibility: Leashed dogs permitted
Fees and permits: None
Schedule: Dawn to dusk
Maps: Go to the US Fish and Wildlife Service website: www .fws.gov/southwest/refuges/ oklahoma/wichitamountains/ brochuresmaps.html.
Trail contacts: Wichita Mountains Wildlife Refuge, 32 Refuge Headquarters, Indiahoma, OK 73552, (580) 429-3222, fax (580) 429-9323. Refuge visitor center is located at the junction of OK 115 and 49.
Special considerations: Be careful as wildlife can be dangerous. Rattlesnakes and copperheads are found in the area. Bison, longhorn cattle, elk, deer, and prairie dogs should be viewed from a safe distance. Do not approach or feed the wildlife. In late summer 2011 a wildfire swept through a portion of the refuge. Much of the grasslands were scorched but started to bounce back immediately with new growth. Wildlife was largely unharmed. WMWR is an

enormous swath of land where there is much to discover and explore beyond the burned areas. **Other:** With 15 miles of designated hiking trails, there are plenty of hiking options for the day hiker or weekend visitor. Check with the visitor center to see if there are special guided hikes or tours. It's possible that you might hear aircraft plane maneuvers overhead during your hike in the refuge as Fort Sill military base is very close to the refuge.

Finding the trailhead: From Oklahoma City drive I-44 south to the Medicine Park/OK 49 exit. Continue on OK 49, going west 10 miles to the refuge gate. Drive OK 49 through the refuge, following signs to left at the French Lake/Dog Run Hollow Trail System sign. Park at the end of the road in the parking area. GPS: N34 43.276' / W98 42.182'

The Hike

Established in 1901, the Wichita Mountains Wildlife Refuge was created mainly to provide a habitat for the endangered American bison that was diminishing rapidly across the plains. Now the refuge serves as a link to the past, where the rangelands of the refuge offer a home to a number of historical legacy species. With the introduction of the vanishing Texas longhorn cattle in 1927 as well as Rocky Mountain elk, white-tailed deer, and, of course, American bison, the mixed-grass prairie provides enough grazing to sustain the large herds. The herd of Texas longhorn cattle number about 300 while the refuge maintains approximately 550 bison.

Start the hike at the trail sign that displays the Dog Run Hollow Trail System Trail Map as it follows the French Lake trailhead. Begin at the Longhorn trail marker that leads left.

Wichita Mountains Wildlife Refuge: Longhorn Trail

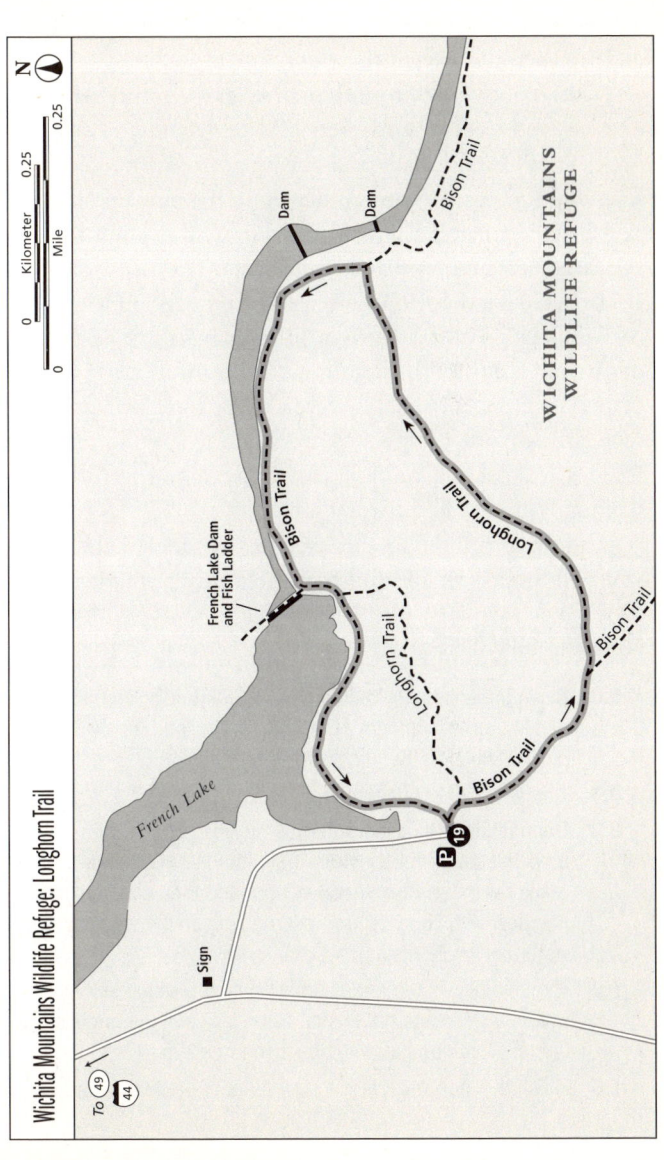

N

0   Kilometer   0.25
0   Mile   0.25

To 49
44

Sign

French Lake

French Lake Dam and Fish Ladder

Bison Trail

Bison Trail

Longhorn Trail

P 19

Bison Trail

Longhorn Trail

Dam

Dam

Bison Trail

WICHITA MOUNTAINS
WILDLIFE REFUGE

If you prefer a longer hike, consider the West Cache Creek and Bison Trails toward the right.

The trail winds around prairie grass, scrub oaks, and cottonwood trees toward French Lake, where you will have good views of the dam and the opportunity to see ducks and wild turkeys. As you ramble along the embankment, the trail becomes parallel with the water. At this point look for the large, spiraling concrete fish ladder. The fish ladder was constructed in the 1930s after the dam was built to allow native species of fish to spawn in French Lake. The fish ladder would aid the fish swimming upstream to cross over the dam into French Lake. However, there were no native fish species that made the journey upstream to spawn in the lake. It does make for a unique site to see along an otherwise seemingly untouched natural area.

Continue following the trail near French Lake, where you will loop back and finish at the trail sign marker.

Miles and Directions

0.0   Begin the Longhorn Trail by crossing the bridge from the parking area. Turn right at the fork where the Longhorn sign is posted. Hike on the flat, packed-dirt path.

0.3   Turn left at the Longhorn fork.

0.8   The trail leads to a fork with trail markers. For the abbreviated version of the Longhorn Trail, turn left and follow the marker with the Bison head symbol and then cuts through a meadow with Longhorn symbol markers until it reaches the waterway where bison markers appear again.

1.2   The trail follows the embankment near the water, where you will be able to see the French Lake dam and the famous fish ladder. Continue following the bison markers.

1.5   Finish the loop back at the start point of the hike.

Oklahoma City Area Outdoor Organizations

The Oklahoma Outdoor Network
http://oklahomaoutdoornetwork.net/

OKC Walking Club
(405) 550-9256

Oklahoma Sierra Club
http://oklahoma.sierraclub.org/outings/index.html

Oklahoma City Audubon Society
http://okc-audubon.org/

About the Author

Gigi Ragland is a freelance journalist specializing in food, travel, and outdoor recreational writing. She is a native Oklahoman who grew up in Oklahoma City. She spent her childhood exploring the creek trails and local parks within the Bethany area where she lived.

What's So Special about Unspoiled, Natural Places?

Beauty   Solitude   Wildness   Freedom   Quiet   Adventure
Serenity   Inspiration   Wonder   Excitement
Relaxation   Challenge

There's a lot to love about our treasured public lands, and the reasons are different for each of us. Whatever your reasons are, the national **Leave No Trace** education program will help you discover special outdoor places, enjoy them, and preserve them—today and for those who follow. By practicing and passing along these simple principles, you can help protect the special places you love from being loved to death.

The Principles of **Leave No Trace**

- Plan ahead and prepare
- Travel and camp on durable surfaces
- Dispose of waste properly
- Leave what you find
- Minimize campfire impacts
- Respect wildlife
- Be considerate of other visitors

Leave No Trace is a national nonprofit organization dedicated to teaching responsible outdoor recreation skills and ethics to everyone who enjoys spending time outdoors.

To learn more or to become a member, please visit us at www.LNT.org or call (800) 332–4100.

Leave No Trace, P.O. Box 997, Boulder, CO 80306